Monkey Business

Are You Controlling Events or Are Events Controlling You?

William Oncken, III

Executive
Excellence
Publishing

For permissions requests, contact the publisher or author:

Executive Excellence Publishing   The William Oncken Corp.
1344 East 1120 South   18601 LBJ FWY, Suite 520
Provo, UT 84606   Mesquite, TX 75150
phone: 1-801-375-4060   phone: 1-972-613-2084
toll free: 1-800-304-9782   fax: 1-972-613-3182
fax: 1-801-377-5960   www.oncken.com
www.eep.com

For Executive Excellence books, magazines and other
products, contact Executive Excellence directly.
Call 1-800-304-9782, fax 1-801-377-5960, or visit our Web
site at www.eep.com.

For products and services of The William Oncken
Corporation, see pages 163-164.

Printed in the United States

10 9 8 7 6 5 4 3 2 1

ISBN: 1-890009-24-5

Library of Congress Catalog Card Number: 99-75865

Illustration by David E. Tripp.

Printed by Publishers Press

This book is a revised and expanded treatment of the edited excerpt of *Managing Management Time*™ that appeared
in the famous November-December 1974 *Harvard
Business Review* article entitled, *Management Time: Who's
Got the Monkey?* The 1974 article has been declared a
"Classic" by the *Review* and is one of their two best-selling
reprints of all time.

Advance Praise for Monkey Business

"*Monkey Business* reflects a real understanding of how organizations and individuals function . . . or perhaps dysfunction. It provides a humorous, insightful look at common management mistakes, along with truly potent methods of freeing up management time. Not pompous, not erudite, just good, practical methods based on common sense."

Peter Strong, Training Manager, UFE, Inc.
(United For Excellence)

"Practical, perceptive, and down-to-earth advice. This book extends and expands the practical framework established by William Oncken, Jr."

Ward Davidson, Vice President of Sales, Paracel

"Most recommendations you get about handling management are either useless or counter-productive. But in *Monkey Business* you get the best advice there is in the universe today."

Paul M. Weyrich, President,
Free Congress Foundation

"Bill Oncken has hit the nail on the head with his highly readable, straight-talking, nifty little book. This is a 'must-read' for managers at any level who are plagued with too many tasks.

David E. Tripp, Illustration—Advertising Design

"Bill Oncken's monkey analogies are wonderful. They help us relate theory to actual workplace relationships. Examples on almost every page provide a comprehensive and helpful way to look at the process of management and leadership. It's practical, easy to understand, and fun to read!"

Rod Rightmire, Ph. D., Professor Emeritus, Indiana University, Coordinator and Moderator of the NATPE (National Association of Television Program Executives) Video Workshops

"As a broadcast manager, I am impressed with the keen insight Bill Oncken, III has into management techniques. As an educator, I appreciate the great lessons *Monkey Business* offers to those who aspire to management positions in our industry."

Lew Klein, President, NATPE Educational Foundation

"I and my colleagues are true believers in the Oncken teachings of managing time and projects within an organization. The delivery of this powerful information is done with humor and contagious energy. It will get your attention, and you will take it seriously!"

Hymie Pogir, Rehab Vice President of Marketing, Powered Products, Invacare Corporation

"As soon as I finished chapter two, I enthusiastically jotted down the following words in the margin: refreshing, clear, entertaining, informative, enlightening, useful. Thanks for making me laugh, think, abandon a few bad habits, and re-institute some good ones."

Fred E. Van Horn, Colonel, U.S. Army, Retired, Executive Vice President, Georgia Military College

"Bill Oncken is on target! Monkey Business is serious management. Public sector, private sector—Monkey Business will get you the discretionary management time you need. Monkey Business stands the test of time . . . your time!"

John Wesley Yoest, Jr, Assistant Secretary of Health and Human Resources, The Commonwealth of Virginia

"I've used the "monkey philosophy" for eight years, and it really works! Monkey Business is an excellent guide to empowering employees and becoming a professional manager."

Martin T. Moor, Manager, Global Business Applications, The Ridge Tool Company

"I think the "monkey" principle is probably the single most important tool we can give managers to increase their effectiveness on the job. This new book, Monkey Business, distills the "monkey" concept down to a quick, unforgettable read, which is easily absorbed and applied. This is the secret weapon managers need to make the transition from "doing" to leading."

Fred W. Hunt, Vice President of Advertising, Star Tribune, Minneapolis Minnesota

"Bill Oncken has done it again! He has effectively converted esoteric management principles into practical action steps by describing how to become a professional manager. Monkey Business is vital for all people in management positions."

Dean Harbry, MIS Director and Principal, Ronald Blue & Co

"Here's the book the television industry has been waiting for. Mr. Oncken provides practical advice on becoming a better manager, coping with change, and creating stability in a time of vast transformations."

Tony Burke, General Manager,
KLCS TV, Los Angeles, CA

"*Monkey Business* was right on target and should be required reading for all aspiring or neophyte managers. It would keep a lot of monkeys with their rightful owners. Seasoned managers could lose a monkey or two and find themselves carrying a lighter load if they read this book."

Jesse Brown,
Secretary of Veteran Affairs, 1993-1997,
Brown and Associates World Wide Consultants,
Alexandria, VA

"Hugely entertaining and incredibly instructive. If you can't attend one of Oncken's "Monkey Schools," you have to read *Monkey Business.*"

R. Jane Brown, President,
Minnesota High Technology Association

"As for the book, I loved it, just as I did the seminar. Oncken's unique and highly effective verbal skills make the reading have even more impact and meaning. For someone like me, who's been around a few decades and been exposed to many management consultants, Oncken's clear-thinking and straightforward approach, frequently mixed with delightful and whimsical humor, is special and priceless."

Richard C. Block,
Block Communications Group,
Santa Monica, CA

Dedication

This book is dedicated to my father, the late William Oncken Jr.(1912-1988).

He graduated from Princeton and pursued graduate studies at Columbia University. In his varied career, he was a physics instructor, geophysicist, Naval Officer, government official, business executive, and management consultant and trainer.

During World War II he served as lieutenant commander, USNR, and after the war—as a civilian—he worked with the Department of the Navy and in the Office of the Chief of Staff, Department of the Army. He enjoyed the distinction of having been appointed an honorary member of the faculties of the U.S. Naval Post Graduate School, U.S. Army Command and General Staff College, and the Industrial College of the Armed Forces. Bill moved from the government to the private sector in 1955, which led to the formation of his own management consulting company in 1960 in New York City. It was during this period that Bill articulated his own leadership and managerial philosophy entitled *Managing Management Time*™, from which the material in this book is derived.

In 1970 he moved his family and corporate office to Dallas, Texas. A gifted, dynamic, and entertaining speaker, Mr. Oncken was for many years a regular lecturer at the management courses of The Presidents' Association and was a favorite faculty member of The Young Presidents' Organization at their National Universities. His unique and inimitable presentations ignited audiences and left them with unforgettable insights and practical solutions to their basic management problems.

Mr. Oncken is best known for his creative genius in originating the *Managing Management Time*™ (or "Get Those Monkeys on the Proper Backs") seminar. This program enjoys international success with all levels of management, and over the years his monkey analogy has become a legend in management circles.

His articles appeared in many professional publications, including one in the *Harvard Business Review* titled "Management Time— Who's Got The Monkey?" This article was an edited excerpt of one segment of the seminar and is one of the two most requested reprints in the history of the *Review*.

Many of today's managers and leaders have said that they owe much of their success to the insights they gained from Bill's work. Hal Burrows and Ken Blanchard, associates of my father, echoed the respect that many felt for him at the time of his death when they wrote:

Bill Oncken, like Amadeus Mozart, was that exceedingly rare combination of masterful composer and virtuoso performer, the difference being that Bill used words instead of musical notes to fashion his works. His masterwork,

Managing Management Time™, *is a timeless, enduring composition that captures the very essence of management, an art as old as organizations themselves. And anyone who ever saw him perform his work will never forget the experience!*

Contents

Foreword

There are three types of laws.

Man-made laws, the result of human legislation, vary from place to place and time to time. Some are wise. Some are foolish. Some are destructive. Some are unworkable and can't ever be enforced. Some only apply to specific categories of people.

Divine laws come from revelation, have general application, and represent an ideal which imperfect humans can at best approximate.

Natural laws are guesses about the nature of reality which are validated through experience. We discover them. They apply to everyone and operate whether we want them to or not.

Natural laws exist before we discover them both in the physical world of matter and energy and in the world of human relations. Successful people tend to be those who study, learn, and use as much as they can of what has been discovered about, simply put, what works and what doesn't work.

We can build and fly an airplane, but we'd get into big trouble if we ignored or forgot the physical laws about how gravity affects all objects.

Similarly, there's a wealth of hard-won, trial-and-error knowledge about the world of human endeavor. Some actions produce better results than others. Those who would lead others in any activity, from politics to business, should seek out and study the best sources of wisdom about what makes someone a successful leader.

About 25 years ago I first attended Bill Oncken's *Managing Management Time*™ seminar. My then-employer, direct marketing leader Richard Viguerie, brought Oncken in each year and required all Viguerie employees to attend his seminar. Oncken was a dazzling speaker. And that helped, because much of what he taught was counterintuitive, a body of management techniques which no one could have thought up spontaneously.

Clearly, Oncken had studied management techniques deeply. Oncken had figured out general rules which, if followed, made as productive as possible the relationship between supervisors and subordinates. Application of Oncken's wisdom helped make Viguerie's company the unchallenged national leader in political direct mail.

Other sources of management principles I've seen are mostly dull and often, I think, wrong. Oncken is never dull and, I believe, always right.

Exposure to the Oncken techniques is a life-changing experience. Once you've learned them, you can't help noticing the success managers have when they use them. And when managers struggle, almost over their heads in a sea of troubles, they aren't applying Oncken's rules.

In the decades since my first Oncken seminar, I have worked as a staffer at the U.S. Senate, on the Reagan White House Staff, and as head of my own educational foundation. I've counseled many people who have created effective organizations. In every case I've seen, those who applied Oncken's principles have had more success as managers than those who didn't.

A few years ago, I learned that the late Bill Oncken's son, William Oncken III, has continued presenting the Oncken seminars.

I hired him to teach the Oncken techniques to my staff and began recruiting others to come to his seminars. Some of the most effective public policy organization leaders in America have thanked me profusely for virtually dragging them to hear young Bill Oncken.

Now he has assembled for wider distribution in this book, *Monkey Business*, the key Oncken principles.

It's all here:

- Management principles.
- Humorous terminology which makes the principles easy to remember.
- Anecdotes which teach why those principles which appear counterintuitive nevertheless really work.

I'm giving all 54 of my staff this book with instructions I can give only as advice to all other readers.

Read this carefully. Then read it again. Think deeply about the principles presented. Everything you hope to achieve in your current job and all future jobs may depend on your understanding and application of this wisdom.

Morton C. Blackwell, President
The Leadership Institute

Ken Blanchard on Bill Oncken Jr.

In the foreword to Bill's classic text, Ken Blanchard described Bill Oncken Jr. and his work this way:

Every once in a while, someone comes along in a field who sees things more clearly and accurately than others in the field. Ted Williams was always considered that kind of hitter in baseball. The reason he hit for a higher average than anyone else was that he seemed to see the ball better. Well, Bill Oncken is that kind of person in the field of management.

The reason Bill Oncken has been consistently in such high demand as a teacher of managers for over 25 years is that he sees what's going on in organizations much more clearly than anyone else in our field. The loud bursts of laughter that continuously echo from his training sessions are sounds of recognition. Since crying in public is not an accepted practice for managers, the only thing left for them to do is laugh.

And laugh they do. Why? Because Bill Oncken, time after time, hits both the absurdities and realities of organizational life with such accuracy that it hurts.

There is one other reason I am excited about *Managing Management Time*—it shows the depth of knowledge Bill Oncken has about managerial and organizational behavior. (While many have) known him for his "monkey-on-the-back" analogy, either from hearing about it in a training session or reading about it in his classic November 1974 *Harvard Business Review* article "Management Time—Who's Got the Monkey?", fewer people know the depth and breadth of Bill Oncken's knowledge and understanding. *Managing Management Time* is not just about time management; it's a complete course in management.

Why is Bill Oncken so insightful? The real reason—he paid the price. He spent over 20 years as a practicing manager before he decided to teach managers. Most management consultants and trainers, including myself, started as academics—students and teachers of management behind the "hallowed halls." While we were getting our lumps trying to publish so we wouldn't perish, Bill was out in the real world learning from experience. While our articles and books might have gotten us promoted, Bill's bruises got him a graduate degree from the "School of Hard Knocks." That is something I have learned to respect. In fact, I think Bill Oncken has probably forgotten more than most people in our field ever knew.

The truths Bill Oncken will give you can set you free and make your organization a more productive and satisfying place for everyone to work.

KENNETH H. BLANCHARD is chairman of Ken Blanchard Companies in Escondido, California. This is taken from the foreword Ken wrote for Bill Oncken Jr.'s masterwork, Managing Management Time, *currently being revised for re-release.*

Acknowledgments

I would like to express my deep appreciation for the support of those who encouraged and assisted me in getting this book ready for publication.

My most important thank-you is to my family: mother, brother John, and sister Inge; without their encouragement and support, this book never would have been written.

I would like to thank Winnie Danley and Jo Annette Bex of my staff for their patience and persistence in helping me not only assemble the material for the first-draft manuscript, but correct and rework the subsequent drafts into what has become the text of the present book.

And thanks also to Dave Tripp, who contributed many hours with me and my staff as we tried our hand at coming up with a cover design that would be engaging and attractive.

Thank you to Jaime Cendra, owner of Advance Design Center Inc., for the use of his facilities, and to Doug Livingston for his creative assistance in bringing color to the book jacket.

Many thanks to Ken Shelton—my editor—for his patience and for providing me with a graduate-level education in the nuances of publishing and professional editing during these many months.

A special thank-you to our clients and friends who took the time to review the manuscript, offering suggestions (many of which were adopted), and for the endorsements they very kindly provided.

Introduction

In any organization, the manager's bosses, peers, and subordinates—in return for their active support—impose some requirements, just as the manager imposes some requirements upon them when they are drawing upon his or her support. These demands constitute so much of the manager's time that successful leadership hinges on the ability to control this "monkey-on-the-back" input effectively.

This dilemma is the basis for the saga of the harried manager, who learns through hard experience to delegate in such a manner that the care and feeding of "monkeys" (the next moves) is always in the hands of staff members. Otherwise, managers will be doing the work of their team members, even as these people are enjoying diversions at the expense of the company and its management.

As you read this tale of *Monkey Business*, you will likely see yourself in the role of the boss, the manager—or perhaps managee—and identify with their particular challenges. In the end, you might make the same sort of resolutions regarding your management of people.

chapter one

Setting the Stage for Success

At the end of every working day, tens of thousands of people, including most managers and leaders, ask themselves a puzzling question: "Where did my time go today?"

Because these dedicated and perceptive people typically want to keep their jobs, they won't risk an honest reply. And yet, upon the answer—and upon the remedy—may hinge the difference between success and failure for managers, employees, and organizations.

Your Role

Managers are men and women whose contributions derive more from their judgment and influence than from their personal time and effort (or labor). While managers constitute a minority of the total population in any given company, they have the most impact on their organization's well-being.

How they manage their time is governed by considerations very different from those governing the management of the time of non-managers—those whose contributions stem primarily from their time and effort.

For non-managers, time management is simply the science and art of "doing more in less time" and consists primarily of nostrums for improved self-organization, mantras for improved self-discipline, and gadgetry for self-measurement and assessment. This approach is suited primarily to such people as salespersons, accountants, industrial engineers, designers, authors, quality-control inspectors, cab drivers, doctors in private practice, entrepreneurs, small farmers, and other professionals whose "bottom line" is the direct result of their independent output. The applicable principle is, "Plan your work, then work your plan."

By contrast, the managers' "bottom line" is the collective result of the outputs of many others, both inside and outside their own organizations, whom they can control only through their judgment and influence. For managers, time management becomes a strategy for maximizing their batting average in the judgments they make and their leverage through the influence they exert.

Managers must first maximize their discretionary time (time needed to reach the necessary judgments) by getting control of the timing and the content of their management time.

Where Does Your Time Go?

Management time relates to the interaction between managers and stakeholders, both inside and outside the organization.

A manager's management time includes, but is not limited to, the following four components:

Boss-imposed time—the time necessary to accomplish those activities which the boss requires and which the manager cannot disregard without direct and swift penalty.

System-imposed time—the time necessary to accommodate the requirements placed on the manager for support from his or her peers. These requirements cannot be ignored lest there be penalties, though not always direct or swift.

Self-imposed time—the time needed to do those things which the manager originates or agrees to do. A certain portion of this kind of time, however, will be taken up by subordinates and is called "subordinate-imposed time." The remaining time will be his or her own and is called "discretionary time." Self-imposed time is not subject to administrative penalty since neither the boss nor the system can discipline the manager for not doing what they did not know the manager had intended to do in the first place. There are very subtle but serious non-administrative penalties suffered by managers who mishandle their self-imposed time, ranging from being inaccessible to their subordinates to having little time for themselves and their families.

Externally-imposed time—the time necessary to meet the needs of customers, investors,
labor, suppliers, government agencies, and com-
munity groups, among others. If we ignore their
requirements, they might ignore us—in which
case the whole ballgame would be over (we can
shut our doors).

The Dilemmas

Boss-imposed and system-imposed time pose
two significant dilemmas for those interested in
making their own work and that of their organization more innovative and effective.

1. Compliance. The boss requires operational
compliance. He or she must comply, or the leadership and accountability structures of the organization fall apart. Some feel that, to get things
done, they must from time to time "overrule" their
boss—be innovative at the risk of being accused of
non-compliance, for which there is no theoretical
basis or model (although the Navy does have a
term for it—*mutiny*).

2. Conformity. The system requires administrative conformity (often perceived as individual
ends thwarted by organizational means).
Individuals in the system must conform, or the
team structure of the enterprise falls apart. Again,
some feel that, to get things done, they must occasionally override the system—be innovative at the
risk of being branded a non-conformist, a perceived necessity for which once more there is no
theoretical model (although there are words for

those who display this amateurish behavior, such as *prima donna, martinet, maverick, free spirit, creative type,* etc.).

3. Innovation. Yet the organization expects and must require innovation upward and sideways in all job categories, or it will fail to be sufficiently adaptive to survive. How can the organization get the innovation it so desperately needs and still maintain both its accountability and its team structures?

In their attempts to resolve these dilemmas, managers are perceived at times to be saying that they want innovation and at other times implying that they cannot tolerate it.

Your Monkey Strategy in a Nutshell

The managing of management time and the generating of discretionary time require managers to get control over the timing and content of what they do. Since what their bosses and the system impose on them are backed by penalty, the proper use of their self-imposed time must become a major concern.

The managers' strategy is to increase the "discretionary" component of their self-imposed time by minimizing or doing away with the "subordinate" component—eliminating "upward delegation." They will then use the added time increment to get better control over their boss-imposed and system-imposed activities by (1) building the boss's confidence in their competence and (2) building a cooperative relationship with their peers and support groups, all of which takes discretionary time.

Most managers spend much more subordinate-imposed time than they even faintly realize. We shall use our "monkey-on-the-back" analogy to examine how subordinate-imposed time comes into being and what the manager can do about it.

Becoming Monkey Savvy

To become monkey savvy, you need to be aware of what a monkey is and who has the monkey.

What is a monkey? A monkey is whatever the next move is when dialogue between two parties breaks off. A monkey is not a problem, project, program, or opportunity; a monkey is simply the next move, the next initiative, the next action step in resolving a problem, moving ahead with a program or project, or capitalizing on an opportunity.

If you think about it, in most of your conversations during working hours, there comes a point where the dialogue breaks off and there is a next move.

Let me explain how our monkey metaphor corresponds to the conventional language of management. When I use the word "monkey," conventional managers use the word "assignment." They define an assignment as "any responsibility that is executable at a given point in time and place." So if I ask you to talk to accounting, it is an assignment. If I ask you to write a letter, that's an assignment. If I ask you to make a phone call, that's an assignment. If I ask you to make a two-day business trip, that's an assignment. Why? Because they're all executable approximately at a given point in time and place. They each correspond, therefore, to my definition of what a "monkey" is, namely a "next move."

Can you now deduce what "gorilla" corresponds to in the language of management? A project. Precisely, because a project is not executable at a given point in time and place. A project is a process consisting of one or more phases.

What, then, is the relationship between projects and assignments? Academia tells us that a project is the vector sum of a lot of a little assignments laid end to end. It all goes back to the Renaissance when they rediscovered the natural law of cause and effect. If you're going to get from here to there, it's got to be via the vector sum of a lot of little "next moves." In my language, I say that a gorilla is the vector sum of a lot of little monkeys laid "nose-to-tail."

Being able to identify monkeys, however, is not enough. You need to know a second important property of monkeys. If you get mixed up on this point, you could easily mishandle monkeys in your care and keeping.

Who has the monkey? For every monkey there are two parties involved—one to work it and the other to supervise it. The critical issue is, who's got that next move? The one who has the next move has the monkey—that's how you know monkeys when you see them.

31

The question of "who has the monkey" must be expressly stated; otherwise, no one knows who has the next move or even what the next move is. This can result is either nothing being done or whatever is done being done by the wrong person. Managers are paid to make sure that the right thing is done by the right person at the right time.

What Is Subordinate-Imposed Time?

Upward-leaping monkeys (next moves that have been upwardly delegated) are manifestations of subordinate-imposed time and can chew up a lot of your discretionary time. Subordinate-imposed time begins the moment a monkey successfully executes a leap from the back of a subordinate to the back of his or her manager, and it does not end until the monkey is returned to its proper owner for care and feeding.

The Oncken Freedom Scale

Our freedom to act varies according to the level of initiative and empowerment we enjoy. A manager can exercise five levels of initiative in relation to the boss and to the system:

(5) **act** on own, then routinely report (highest);

(4) **act,** but advise "at once" ("at once" means anything more frequent than "routine");

(3) **recommend,** then take resulting action;

(2) **ask** what to do;

(1) **wait** until told (lowest initiative).

When your people operate at Freedom Levels 1 and 2, they create subordinate-imposed time for you—time you must spend doing their thinking, planning, and problem solving for them. It is time imposed on you by your staff. It takes discretionary time—your discretionary time—to do this.

When subordinates operate at Freedom Levels 1 and 2, they are like anchors around your neck, whereas at Freedom Level 3 several positive things are happening simultaneously: you are engaging their brains; they are beginning to self-actualize; they are learning the twin arts of formulating and selling their ideas; and as they successfully sell you on their recommendations, you are gaining confidence in their abilities.

Their proven track record over time will allow you to delegate responsibility to them—allowing them to operate at Freedom Levels 4 and 5. They win because at the high end of the Freedom Scale, they are self-managing or self-directing—albeit within the guidelines you have set. You win because you are having to spend less of your discretionary time in supervisory interactions with your subordinates.

In the following chapters, we will examine the causes of and the remedies for subordinate-imposed time.

chapter two

Are You a Magnet for Monkeys?

Each of us has a finite amount of self-imposed time, and often most of it is subordinate-imposed—time we spend answering their questions and thinking up things for them to do. That's why we have little discretionary time. Those who master the process of eliminating subordinate-imposed time will maximize the discretionary time available to them for their priorities both on and off the job.

If we don't reduce—if not eliminate—our subordinate-imposed time, we could become part of a university research study entitled: "Why are managers typically running out of time while their subordinates are typically running out of work?" To answer that golden question, I will give you a situational definition of a monkey by describing several events that all managers encounter at some time during their working day.

Situation 1: "Let Me Think It Over, and I'll Let You Know."

Suppose it is ten o'clock Monday morning, and you are walking down the hallway on a discretionary mission—something of real merit you have chosen to do.

I don't know how you found the discretionary time, management being what it is, but the reason you are on this discretionary mission is that you have many desirable executive traits: you are widely known throughout the company as a person of creativity, originality, imagination, innovation, zeal, leadership, and guts. These are the things that create discretionary time.

As you proceed down the hallway, whom do you see at the other end coming in your direction but George. George works for you, and when the two of you meet in the hallway, he says to you, "Good morning, boss. By the way, we've got a problem."

That remark stops you dead in your tracks. You've never been known to walk away from a problem. That's one of the reasons you were promoted into the job you've got right now. In fact, your boss has frequently complimented you by saying, "You are a flypaper for problems."

So you stand there transfixed in the hallway as George disembowels the problem all over the floor in front of you. You listen as he goes through, in excruciating detail, the crisis that now confronts him.

Why are you listening? Because you had his job once. That's why you feel far more adequate to solve his problems than you do your own. You feel far more familiar with his problems than you do with your own; working with his problem gives you a holiday from working on your own. So with all of those temptations in your path, you stand there to see if you can try to help him solve his problem. Moreover, you have a very humanitarian attitude. You feel he is entitled at least once in a while to watch genius (you) at work, a fringe benefit that comes with his job.

As he talks, you find yourself getting embroiled and finally sucked into the vortex of the problem, and you recognize in this problem the same two characteristics common to all the problems that members of your staff gratuitously bring to your attention:

You know enough to get involved,
but not enough to make the on-the-spot
decision expected of you.

After what seems to be only five minutes, you look at your watch and see that, lo and behold, 30 minutes have gone by. So you say to him, "Wait a minute, George. Thirty minutes have gone by. I was on my way someplace. I'm late already. This is a very important problem, and we've only scratched the surface. We can't deal with it any more now. We'll have to have a decision, but this will require further thought. So, I'll tell you what we'll do. Let me think it over, and I'll let you know." The two of you then part company.

Let's examine that incident and see what really happened there. First, before you and George encountered each other in the hallway, who had the monkey on his back? George, obviously. It couldn't have been on your back; you didn't even know there was one. Then, 30 minutes later you said to him, "Let me think it over, and I'll get back to you." And he said, "That's fine with me." Now, as you part company, who has the monkey on his back? You do!

Subordinate-Imposed Time Revisited

One of the principal enemies of discretionary time is subordinate-imposed time. Subordinate-imposed time for you begins the instant the monkey executes a successful leap from your staff member's back to your back, and it does not end until the monkey is returned to its proper owner for care and feeding.

In accepting the monkey, you voluntarily assumed a position subordinate to your staff member. You have allowed George to make you his subordinate by doing two things a subordinate is expected to do for the boss: 1) you have accepted the responsibility from him, and 2) you have promised him a progress report.

Recall the second half of our monkey definition:

For every monkey there are ONLY two parties involved, namely one to work it and one to supervise it.

Now, where's the monkey? On your back. Which role do you have? The worker role. Which role does George have? The supervisory role—the only role left on the table for him to pick up.

To make sure you do not miss this point, he will later stick his head in your office and cheerily query, "How's it coming, boss?" This query takes other forms such as:

> "Time's a-wasting!"
> "When are you gonna do it?"
> "Hey, boss, gotta fish or cut bait!"
> "When are we going to get action?"
> "When are we going to get a decision?"
> "When are you going to make up your mind?"

Upside-Down Management

This form of "supervision" is really a form of perversion. It's upside-down management, a perverted pyramid where the managee manages the manager.

"How's it coming?" is a technical term that identifies who has the supervisory role. During working hours, when two managers encounter each other in the hallway and one of them says to the other, "How's it coming?", you know that the boss is the person who is asking the question. This may have no bearing on how the organization is structured, but it directly describes the current reality. The person who accepts the monkey is, by definition, the worker.

Why do executives post organization charts on office walls? To explain to people how the company is supposed to run and to let everybody know who is working for whom. But as soon as these charts are posted, managers walk around saying to people, *"Let me think it over, and I'll let you know."* That innocent statement gives the boss the worker role, and it gives a subordinate the supervisory role. As a result we see hourly workers supervising their front-line managers, who in turn supervise general managers, who supervise vice presidents, and the vice presidents supervise the president. Under such a system, the president would have all the monkeys! Ridiculous!

The whole organization is turned upside down, inside out, all crossed up, and entirely contrary to how the corporation intended it to be when they posted organization charts on the walls. Based on current operations, the president should join a union, and the hourly worker should be elevated to the Board of Directors. If the shareholders ever found out that this is what's going on, they would raise havoc at the annual shareholders' meeting by saying, "That's not how it was explained to us."

This exchange of monkeys is all being done voluntarily up and down the line, in complete contradiction to the intention expressed in the organization chart. Consider this: How can one person (the president) have 5,000 bosses down the line and possibly do anything for anybody?

So we've got to get straight who's got the worker role and who's got the supervisory role, with regard to every next move, and keep it straight.

Situation 2: "Send Me a Memo on That."

In concluding a working conference with a member of my staff, Mike, my parting words are, "Fine. Send me a memo on that."

Note that the monkey is now on my subordinate's back because the next move is his, but it is poised for a leap. Watch the monkey. Mike dutifully writes the memo and emails it. Soon, I see it on my computer mailbox and read it. Whose move is it now? Mine. If I do not make that move soon, I will get a follow-up memo from him (another form of supervision!).

Managee's Frustration with Manager

As Mike persistently seeks my reactions to his memos, I increasingly resort to evasive maneuvers. He now coins a nickname for me and injects it into the rumor mill: "Dead-letter Oncken." Then he'll often add, "Doesn't he ever read anything? At least he could give you the courtesy of a reply. He says he wants our ideas! Right now I've got a half a dozen money-making projects on hold. I can't move ahead on them until he gives me the green light."

The longer I delay, the more frustrated Mike becomes as he is simply "spinning his wheels," and the more guilty I feel as my backlog of subordinate-imposed time mounts.

When my evasive tactics fail and Mike finally corners me, I find that his questions have become more sophisticated. He sits down by my desk and says, "Oncken, we must either fish or cut bait. We've got nine projects on the back burners right now. I can't get any of them off the ground without your approval. When are you going to make up your mind?" I made the mistake of asking him, "Which nine projects are you talking about?" He knows—numbers 1, 5, 15, 18, 24, etc. I didn't even know they were numbered! I still haven't finished reading the memo I got a week ago, let alone the one after that and the one after that. I never asked for this, but because I'm an "amateur" manager, I think I'm obligated to read this, and that's why I am behind.

And Mike is not the only one playing this game. During working hours, our staffs can send us dozens of messages and reports (via email, voice-mail, hard copy, etc.) that put us farther behind all the time.

Remember the good old days, before you had anybody "helping" you? You were caught up. Well, now you have dozens of these monkeys and gorillas. You carry them back and forth between home and office in your briefcase, hoping to get to them.

Situation 3: "Just Let Me Know How I Can Help."

Suppose, once again, that at a meeting with another staff member, Valerie, I agree to provide all the necessary backing for a public relations proposal I have just asked her to develop. My parting words to her are, "Just let me know how I can help."

Here again, the monkey is initially on her back. But for how long? Valerie realizes that she cannot "let me know" until her proposal has my approval.

From experience, she also realizes that her proposal will likely be sitting in my briefcase for weeks, waiting for me to eventually get to it. Who's really got the monkey? Who is supervising whom? Wheel-spinning and bottlenecking are happening again.

chapter three

Monkey "Intelligence"

One of the reasons managers accumulate menageries of monkeys is that—during an already busy day—they do not realize how these monkeys manage to climb on their backs in the first place. So let's begin to peel the onion back and analyze the how and the where of upward-leaping monkeys, and their adverse effects.

Monkey Harpoons. When you pick up "monkeys," what tools do you use? Everyone has their own unique monkey harpoon. These things come in various shapes and sizes. Many managers carry around fancy planners; others prefer electronic organizers; still others have notebooks—anything to jog their memories. When you open these planners, you find a page entitled "Things To Do." Things for whom to do? You! That makes these various time and life management tools little more than "monkey harpoons."

Ambush Sites. Where do you pick up monkeys? You pick up only one or two monkeys a day from George, but you also pick up monkeys daily from many of your other staff members because you are an inveterate, compulsive monkey picker-upper. You don't just pick them up through telephone and computer connections and in hallways, you pick them up in stairwells, elevator shafts, parking lots, cafeteria lines, washrooms, workstations—everywhere but in your own office. That's where you keep them. You accumulate monkeys by the dozens without even realizing it. By the end of the day, you've got a desktop, perhaps even a laptop computer, crawling with monkeys.

Upward-Leaping Monkeys Are Procrastination Prone

Whenever you return to your office after a brief absence, what do you find? You discover that while you were away picking up monkeys from your subordinates, your boss was not idle. Your boss is continuously pregnant with monkeys. Right now he's working on twins, triplets and quadruplets. So in your in-basket, mail slot, or email file, you find a menagerie of monkeys from your boss—messages marked, "See me," or "What's this?" or "Please handle," or "Follow up."

So now you have a day's work from your boss, a day's work from your staff—and there are not enough hours in the day to work off both sets of obligations. I ask you, which of those two sets of monkeys will have higher priority, regardless of the merits of the issues involved? You probably have pictures on your desk of your loved ones.

You have a keen sense of stewardship. Which of these two sets of obligations have priority, regardless of the merits of the issues involved? The boss's monkeys will, of course, take precedence, and other things (other monkeys) will have to wait. However trivial the boss's monkeys may be, they receive attention first.

If you are still confused, consider this: Anything that you fail to do that you promised your subordinates you would do is called **procrastination.** However, anything that you fail to do that your boss wants you to do is not called procrastination—it's a much weightier matter, **insubordination.** If you are a career-oriented, prudent manager and you have to choose between procrastination or insubordination, which will it be? You'd choose procrastination over insubordination any day, and that is why upward-leaping monkeys are prone to procrastination.

How do you get rid of procrastination? Very simple: just pick up all the monkeys your subordinates gladly give you to do, which if you do nothing about them will make you guilty of procrastination, and put them on the backs of your subordinates, who if they do nothing, will be guilty of insubordination.

A Stumbling Block to Becoming a Leader

If this is the way a *professional* manager makes things happen and keeps the monkeys from starving to death through procrastination, why then don't more managers practice this simple management principle with their staffs more often?

In modern management literature, the word "insubordination" is strangely absent in referring to relationships at the management level. At the hourly worker level and in the military, we talk about insubordination, but at the management level we are supposed to be very polite. We work with each other. We are associates. The status differential is distasteful. Behavioral theorists don't like it. But when you deny reality, you deserve the punishment that reality will bring. Insubordination is an essential element in manager-managee (leader-staff) relationships; without it you are missing an essential element.

"We" Is Killing "Us"

How does subordinate-imposed time develop? Why do monkeys leap upward so insidiously, so invisibly, so intangibly? Why do managers pick them up without realizing it? It's because of the way the monkey starts its leap. You're walking down the hallway, and George says to you, "Hi, boss. We've got a problem." Do you get that "we"?

George knew precisely what he was doing. By starting off with "we," he eased you into thinking that the matter under consideration was a joint problem. In other words, he arranged for the monkey to begin its career astride both your backs—one foot on yours and one foot on his. George knew that when the conversation ended, all that monkey had to do was lift the wrong leg, and he, George, would deftly disappear, leaving you alone with another acquisition to your monkey menagerie. That's how quickly and subtly the transfer of responsibility and accountability happens. That's what this "we" stuff does, and that's why this "we" business is crippling organizations worldwide.

chapter four

Whose Monkey Is It Anyway?

There are two ways to avoid the plight of taking on other people's monkeys. One is to train monkeys not to lift the wrong leg, but the better way is not to permit them to put even one foot on your back in the first place.

"We" Don't Have a Problem

Suppose you've got four people reporting to you. That makes a nice little team, and you're the team "coach," leader," or "mentor."

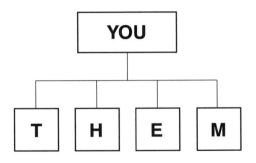

My Team

There's only one person among the five of you who is in a position to speak for the entire team and say, "We've got a problem." Who is that person? You. So when one of your team members says to you, "Boss, we've got a problem," he or she is guilty of a presumptive form of address. Your subordinates are in no position to speak for the whole team and say, "We've got a problem."

Incidentally, when your people come to you with problems, in most cases they are not looking for solutions. They are looking for a problem solver.

The only proper form of address from a subordinate to a manager is, "I've got a problem." It is presumptive for subordinates to say, "We've got a problem." Why? Because they can't speak for the boss. The boss is the captain of a team of which they are members. It is not "our" problem until the boss says it is. Until the boss says, "We've got a problem," the problem is the subordinate's. Both of the monkey's feet shall be firmly placed on the subordinate's back until it has been determined to be otherwise.

Therefore, when team members bring a problem to your attention, which question shall be settled first—**what is it?** or **who has it?** Who has it. If they think the problem is yours, then on whom is the burden of proof? You or them? The burden of proof is always theirs, and if they cannot prove the problem is yours, whose is it now by default? Theirs. That is why you don't have to delegate the problem because you never had it to begin with. The best way not to have a problem in delegation is not to have anything to delegate. Most managers find delegation enormously difficult. Why? They go around all day getting undelegated. Then they've got to reverse the process. To tear a monkey that does not belong there off your back and put it on a subordinate's back where it belongs is as painful as pulling adhesive tape off a hairy leg. Don't go through the agony! If you don't let the monkey leap, you don't have to give it back.

I can imagine what you're thinking, and I can guess what's going to happen tomorrow morning. Some of your subordinates have made a patsy out of you, and you know who they are. You can't wait until you get back to the office tomorrow morning to give one of those people a chance to put some monkeys on your back, just as they always have done.

As you walk down the hall, you encounter Dave. You're ready for him because he has delegated upward before. He says to you, "Hi, boss. We've got a problem."

You stop him right there and say, "What did you say, Dave." He replies, "Boss, we've got a problem."

You continue, "Dave, *we* have never had a problem. In fact, *we* don't have one now; and if I've got anything to do with it, *we* will never again have one. Now, that does not mean that one does not exist. Of course one exists, or you would not have brought it up. You're worth your weight in gold in raising problems, and I want you to continue to do so. I'm perfectly willing to spend all the time necessary to discuss the problem with you.

"But right here in the hallway, the first item on our agenda is for you and me to find out whose problem this is—yours or mine. If it is yours, I'll do everything I can to help you with it. If it is mine, I'm sure you'll do everything you can to help me with it. But no matter which way it comes out, the next move will be yours."

Now he wonders why he brought it up!

If he had known you would be so generous with your time, but that the next move would be his, he could have calculated in advance what that next move inevitably would be. Therefore, he wouldn't bother stopping you in the hallway. He'd be making that move now—at Freedom Level 3, unless otherwise directed.

Why do people bring us their problems? Because if they perceive their boss to be a patsy— a flypaper for problems—their attitude is, "Let him pick them up," and they are off scot free. This is not meant to imply that people are ornery, but they are enormously tempted to let the boss pick up their monkeys.

Professional Monkey Management

To illustrate that point, I'll repeat the little hallway incident with George. This time I'll play it like a professional manager. As he and I encounter each other in the hallway, the monkey tries to leap. But with the precision of a professional manager, I will smack that little monkey right back to where it came from.

So George meets me in the hallway, and he says, "Hi, Oncken. We've got a problem." I don't make an issue of the "we" for now; I'll take care of that later. So for 30 minutes we discuss the problem in the hallway. At the end of the 30 minutes, I say, "George, I don't know where the time went, but I've got to go. We've barely scratched the surface on this thing. This will require further thought."

In this case, the monkey is very elusive, very intangible—further thought!

"George, I can only think of two people in this organization who might give this matter the required further thought—you and me. Now, since I am the boss, you will give this matter the required further thought. Therefore, be back in my office at 4:30 this afternoon with your further thoughts wrapped in marketable form, taking into full account my buying habits."

Where did I put him on the Freedom Scale? Level 3—make a recommendation, and then carry out the action resulting from the dialogue with me.

Where is the monkey now? On his back. Who has the worker role? He has. Which role do I have? The supervisory role.

That is why this afternoon around two o'clock, I'll walk down the hallway—I've got time for this because I haven't got any subordinate-imposed monkeys—stick my head in his office, and say, "Hi, George. How are you coming with your monkey?"

Remember, "how's it coming" identifies who has the management role, just in case he forgets.

Now, if he is not in my office this afternoon at 4:30, we can call that insubordination because it is not unreasonable to require that a subordinate show up, with something. If he is in my office at 4:30, but with no thoughts, we call that insubordination because it is not unreasonable to require that he have a thought. It might be unreasonable, at this stage, to require that he have a good thought. That might be downright unreasonable, but it's not unreasonable to require that he have one thought at 4:30.

Therefore, because he's got a picture on his desk of a lovely wife and three beautiful children, what are the odds that he will be wantonly insubordinate? Almost zero. But if I tell him, "Let me think it over, and I'll let you know," what are the odds that I—as an amateur manager—will have any thought myself by 4:30? Almost zero. So now we are way ahead of the game on this thing.

Remember our definition of a monkey: *A monkey is whatever the next move is when dialogue between two parties breaks off.*

So the subordinate always ends up with the next move, no matter whose problem it may be. This is very important for two reasons.

First, by having subordinates discipline themselves in saying, "I've got a problem," you automatically facilitate your ability to delegate. Because if they say, "We've got a problem," you can't delegate until you undo the part of the problem you've got and give it back to them. But if they start out with "I've got a problem," delegation becomes very easy. You simply keep it that way.

chapter five

Monkey Mismanagement

Monkey mismanagement becomes "life-threatening" when a manager accumulates large quantities of upward-leaping monkeys.

Who Is Working for Whom?

Suppose I have four subordinates who are unique in the fact that they are sensitive about my time requirements, so they have made a pact among themselves not to permit any more than three monkeys a day to leap—whether by phone call, fax, email, memo, or personal encounter—from their backs to mine. This is amazing self-restraint on their part. Let's further suppose that I start out the week with a clean slate. With three monkeys apiece leaping from each of their backs to mine, by the end of the first day (Monday), I've accumulated 12 screaming monkeys, and each monkey will consume some of my time.

Each of these monkeys represents a commitment of time. When you say to a subordinate, "Let me think it over, and I'll let you know," do you calculate how long it will take you to work off that commitment? No. Because "further thought" is a highly intangible, subjective, effervescent thing. We rarely think of "further thought" as being a concrete next move that takes a finite amount of calculable time. That's why it's easy to make these commitments.

Now, suppose that the average work-off time for each of these monkeys is about 30 minutes. Having picked up these monkeys from my staff, I have committed myself to six hours of subordinate-imposed time.

Deteriorating Relationships

Let us suppose on top of this that I am the complete amateur manager, meaning that I am being interrupted by my boss all day long and being thwarted by the system. I am not getting very much done because I have to find some authority in writing somewhere before I can do it. This forces me to go "to the top" for the support I need, and so I have just about worn out my welcome there. Also, I'm a compulsive monkey-picker-upper, at the rate of 12 a day. The life I'm living shouldn't happen even to your worst enemy. There's no salary that could compensate me for the damage that's being done to my nervous system to live a life of being micro-managed by my boss, thwarted by the system, and crippled by my subordinates.

There aren't enough hours in the day to handle all of this. And so with 12 monkeys on my desk at 4:30 p.m. Monday, I decide I've got to get organized. I buy a book entitled *The Management of Time,* which is written by a college professor. He says the first thing you want to do is set priorities. So I take these dozen monkeys and start stacking them in a priority heap, the top priority monkey at the top and the bottom priority monkey at the bottom. I only get halfway through this process, since I'm still harassed by the boss and still thwarted by the system. I sweep those monkeys into my monkey cage, otherwise known as my briefcase, and take them home so I can work on them in the quietude of my den. But when I arrive home, my wife is on the doorstep to greet me. She says, "Bill, you're home just in time to get cleaned up." I say, "Cleaned up for what?" She says, "Have you forgotten again? It's our wedding anniversary." And I think to myself, "Oh, another evening shot to pieces."

The next morning (Tuesday) I trundle "them" back to work for another day of harassment by the boss, frustration with the system, and the acquisition of 12 more monkeys from my subordinates. I try to stack the 24 monkeys in a new priority pyramid, but I am defeated by the ambiguities. With 24 monkeys, I find it impossible to discriminate between what should be priority five and priority six, for example, or even between 14 and 15.

Fortunately, in Chapter 2 of the time management book, the professor anticipated this problem.

He wrote, "When the monkey population is large, what you want to do is to grab three, four, or five monkeys that look alike and talk to each other, and put them in one pile. Grab another three, four, or five monkeys that look alike and talk to each other, and put them in another pile. If you keep that up long enough, you'll have four or five piles, and then stack the piles in priorities (that number is sufficiently small for meaningful discrimination)."

But as I stack these piles in priorities, I get a funny feeling in the pit of my stomach that I'm getting farther and farther away from any one monkey (the actual work) and closer and closer to the abstractions of subject matter classification, so valuable to those who are writing business books, but no good for a manager who's got to get a job done.

So once more I throw all the monkeys into my monkey cage and take them home, hoping I can work on them this evening. But this time I'm greeted on my front doorstep by my creditors in the other roles I play in life, namely, father, neighbor, citizen, church member, etc.

- My seven-year-old daughter, I am advised by my wife, is having a Brownie point pinned on her at 6:30 tonight. The photographer from the local newspaper will be there to document the event for tomorrow morning's edition. There is no way I can duck out of this.

- My wife adds that the church consistory is meeting tonight, and as treasurer I must attend to explain how the extension to the

Sunday School building was constructed without funds.

- Moreover, the local political action group I helped organize about a year ago to "throw the thieves out of office" is going to meet tonight, too. Being a charter member and founder, I must be there.

I am thus paying off my creditors in the other roles I play in life so that when I settle with the last one in line, the undertaker, I'll be solvent forever. And that, they tell me, is what heaven is all about!

- That evening I pin the Brownie point on my daughter.

- And then I rush to the church meeting, where I say, "Brethren, I haven't time to spend with you tonight; but let me say in all earnestness that my prayers are with you and that any decisions you make I'll back to the hilt. If you need help, don't hesitate to call on me."

- With that I'm off to the next meeting.

- And then to the next. And the next.

Thursday morning I dump those 36 monkeys on my desk, but once again—while harassed by the boss and thwarted by the system—I pick up 12 more monkeys from my subordinates for a cumulative total of 48.

The Fate of the Compulsive Monkey-Picker-Upper

But Friday is different. On Fridays I always get delivery of my last monkeys of the week at noon because my subordinates like to clean off their desks so they can get a running start for the weekend.

As I sit there I notice that, my briefcase having snapped open, my monkeys have escaped. I had 60 of them. They don't fit on my desk anymore, they're falling over the side. I'm watching them play tag with each other back and forth across my office floor. They're climbing up and down the walls and hanging from the light fixtures. I'm trying to chase these little creatures down. For every three of them I catch, I lose two. If somebody asked me, "Oncken, what is your monkey inventory—how many do you have?" I would have to say, "I've got about 20, give or take 30, which is a rough count." But even as I gather them up, I haven't got the discretionary time to work them off.

I say to myself, "Oncken, you've got to do something about this. You're never going to make those decisions; you're never going to read all those reports, faxes, emails, and memos; you're never going to do all these things."

About 2:30 p.m. on Friday, I decide to analyze what my problem is. I realize I need privacy, but my door is open. People are walking in and out as if my office were Grand Central Station, the telephone is ringing "off the wall," and my beeper is in a constant state of agitation. So I get up and I walk to my office door, kick it shut, bolt it from the inside so I can get some privacy. I'd love to jerk the batteries out of my beeper and tear my telephone out of the wall by its roots, but I don't think I can get away with that. When I sit back down behind my desk, I call my secretary and say, "Sue, I need privacy for the rest of the day. Therefore, I don't want to see anybody except 'you know who'; I don't want to talk to anybody except 'you know who.'"

Who are the "you know who's"? Anyone who can either make me or break me in a key area of my job.

- For example, my boss, or anyone else in the company who has the clout to enter my office without knocking.

- Or a key customer or client who wants to see me. Shall my secretary say to the customer, "Sorry, Mr. Oncken has no time for customers. He has work to do. Ha, ha, ha."? Will the customer get in? You bet.

Suppose there are 40 key people, inside and outside the company, who have "make or break" clout over my job, and my four subordinates are part of that 40. My shut door will only keep out whom? My subordinates. However, if I've got four staff members out of a population of 40 critical people, my shut door will only keep out 10 percent of the entire threatening population, and 10 percent is too insignificant a figure to have any meaning at all. That is why, in management, a "shut door" during working hours is a snare and a delusion. There is no such thing!

Sue calls me at about 4 p.m. and says, "Mr. Oncken, I'd like you to know that George, Mike, Valerie, and Dave are sitting outside your office urgently wanting to see you before quitting time."

But then I say, "Sue, you say they've been sitting there two hours already? Tell me, what have they been doing all this time?"

She says, "They have been playing computer games, and they're at it now."

I think to myself, "Why don't people take initiative and assume responsibility around here? I worship at the shrine of Douglas MacGregor, who once said that people would rather assume responsibility than not, that people would rather take initiative than not. But Douglas MacGregor never would have written that if he'd had the people working for him that I've got working for me, sitting outside my office, playing games during working hours. If the leadership will behave this way, God help the common working man. The values of our society are coming apart at the very seams!"

"I was formed in the crucible of the Depression. I learned the value of a dollar and the dignity of hard work. Horatio Alger, Andrew Carnegie, and Henry Ford were my great idols, and they were what made America great—not these folks here."

But why are they out there? Earlier this afternoon, right after lunch, they came back to their desks and, being as how it was Friday afternoon, they got to thinking about what they were going to do over the weekend. When they were done thinking about that, their minds turned to Monday, and they decided that, with a couple of hours left, they'd plan their work and get organized for Monday. But then, when they looked at their desks, they discovered they had nothing left to organize. Over the past several days and weeks, they had surrendered to me every significant initiative (next move) in their jobs. Having no significant initiatives left to take, they were unable to get organized. That's why they're sitting outside my office. They want their monkeys back—not to work on, of course. They're sitting out there playing games, fulfilling their supervisory roles! If I gave them half a chance, they would spring into action with:

"Hey, boss, how's it coming?"
"Gotta fish or cut bait!"
"Time's a-wasting!"
"When are you gonna do it?"
"When are we going to get action?"
"When are we going to get a decision?"

And when I have all of their monkeys, they are working in the "dungeon of the prison house of management." They are, in fact, "waiting to be told." My subordinates have lost control of both the timing and content of the work they do, and they don't like it.

Psychologists tell us when you have no initiatives left to take, you are frustrated. Games, they say, are very good antidotes to frustration, so games are what they play during working hours just to keep from going stark, raving mad.

Meanwhile, here I am, evading my staff, inaccessible behind my closed door, overcome with guilt because I owe them all these things. We are like five drowning executives in a death clutch in the middle of the management sea, dragging each other downward.

If I could overhear what they are saying outside the office, I would contemplate acts of murder. Valerie, pointing toward my closed door, is saying, "That man never could make a decision. We should call him 'Bottleneck Oncken.' How anybody ever got that high in our company without making a decision, I'll never know. Just another example of how mediocrity inevitably sinks to the top." Here I am a hard-working, loyal member of our company, working myself to the bone 24 hours a day and all night besides. They're out there playing games, calling me mediocre. Our society is going to pieces.

Benjamin Franklin's grandfather once said that if you want to turn a friend into an enemy, the quickest and simplest way to do it is to become indebted to him. That's why he recommended that you never borrow from your friends, so you won't be indebted to them.

I owe my staff considered responses to so many questions, recommendations, and suggestions that I'm never going to meet my payments. That's why I now think of them as enemies.

Obviously, the reason I'm not able to make any of these "next moves" is that my time is eaten up in meeting my own boss-imposed and system-imposed requirements. To meet these commitments, I need discretionary time, currently denied me because I am preoccupied with all these monkeys. I'm caught in a vicious circle.

How can one be "preoccupied" with something and get nothing done? If any boss is making promises, such as:

- *"I'll think it over and let you know,"* or
- *"I'll see ole So-n-So and get back to you,"* or
- *"Let me read your report, and I'll give you a reply,"*

what are the chances he or she is going to make good on those promises? Extremely small.

If bosses are making promises like that to several people, and they're the only ones who can work them off, those promises are in competition with the monkeys they get from their bosses, the system, and key clients and customers. NO boss is going to live up to those promises, no matter how well-intentioned he or she may be.

It is now Friday at 5 p.m. I've got so many monkeys on my back that the combination of evasion and overwork can no longer stave off the inevitable moment of truth. Today, I must decide. I can think of only two alternatives, amateur manager that I am:

(1) somehow generate some discretionary time, or

(2) take an early retirement, which I can ill afford.

My mind goes back a number of years ago when my company sent me to a one-day course conducted by a reputable consultant entitled "Problem Solving for Managers." The consultant said, "Managers typically jump to solutions before thoroughly analyzing and defining the problem." He showed us the horrible consequences of that approach. "In management," said he, "99 percent of problem solving lies in problem analysis and problem definition. Therefore, if you spend your time on analysis and definition, the solution will fall into place effortlessly." Now that my back is up against the wall, I decide to use what he said even if it kills me. The professor said, "Get out a pen and paper, and when you've defined the problem, you just watch and see whether the solution doesn't just spring forth from the paper itself."

After 15 minutes of racking my brain, it dawns on me now that my problem is this: "I Am Behind." Now, to show you how simple and obvious the solution is, once you've formulated the problem, there is only one conceivable solution, and that is: "Get Caught Up."

I decide, therefore, that I am going to have to get caught up. But how? I choose the very obvious way of coming to the office over the weekend to:

- Make the 16 decisions that are holding up George. Then I can call him into my office on Monday morning and snap these decisions off to him with the precision of a drill sergeant. He will leave my office a released individual walking on cloud nine, highly motivated to do his job;

- Read every one of Mike's progress reports and come up with a definitive response to everything he asked me. I'll call him into my office, snap them off to him with unambiguous precision, so he, too, will leave my office a new individual, walking on cloud nine to do his job;

- and I'll take a similar approach with Valerie and Dave.

It is now six o'clock. Time to go home. Well, how am I going to go home? The usual way would be, of course, to walk out my office door, down the hallway, and down the stairs to the parking lot. But if I do that, I'll pass these people as I go.

Again, with respect to these 60 screaming monkeys in my briefcase, who has the supervisory role? They do. Who has the worker role? I have. And what will they say to me as I walk by?

"Get off the dime."
"Gotta fish or cut bait."
"Gotta get some decisions."
"Hi, boss. How's it coming?"

Why will they say these things? Because they are completely immobilized by having surrendered to me all of their initiatives and next moves. But I, as an amateur manager, don't understand that. All I know is that if I walk past that gauntlet, I would feel guilty just to look at them. On top of that, a half dozen monkeys would leap upon me while I'm walking by, and I wouldn't know I had them until I got home.

So instead of walking past that gauntlet, I slip out the rear exit like an escaping convict to the parking lot, jump in the car, and drive home.

As I drive home, I ponder another point. How can I ever reduce the monkey population when I don't even know how I attracted so many in the first place?

My situation is very clear to everyone but me. Here I am, a hard-working, loyal, devoted member of this company, working under the able supervision of four "managers" who are constantly asking me to be accountable for the things that they have given me to do. They have mastered the twin arts of assigning work and the more difficult art of follow up ("How's it coming?"). That's the situation, but I don't see it yet!

A sleepless night ensues, followed by the most tragic scene of all.

The following morning right after breakfast, I grab my monkey cage (my briefcase) and, saying nothing to my wife, I head for the garage. She, sensing what I'm about to do, rushes after me and, with tears in her voice, says, "Bill! It's another weekend. Must it always be thus?" Flicking a tear from my own eye, I shout, "Honey, you know it's all for you and the kids."

As I walk to my car, I overhear my youngest daughter ask my wife: "Mommy, if Daddy can't get all of his work done during the week, can't they put him in a slow group—like at school?"

I climb into my car and drive to work. My car is the only one in the parking lot that Saturday morning. I walk into the building and down the hallway. Never do my footsteps echo more loudly from one end of that abandoned building to the other than they echo this Saturday morning. Never does my briefcase weigh more than it weighs this Saturday morning. I dutifully walk into my office, lay my briefcase upon my desk, snap open the lid, and survey what I have to do.

chapter six

Conversion from Amateur to Professional Monkey Manager

Before I get down to work, I lift up my eyes and look out the window to gaze for a brief moment at that golf course across the street, drinking in that beautiful sight, wishing I was there. As my eyes rest upon the first tee, whom do I see there teeing off? George, Mike, Valerie, and Dave.

If I could wing my way out of my office window and fly above their heads, I would overhear their conversation. Pointing toward the parking lot, they'd say, "Hey, things are finally looking up. It looks like Bill Oncken has finally decided to earn his money." Spoken like true managers about a hard-working employee who's finally decided to do an honest day's work for a fair day's pay!

Why do they think this way? Simply because they have taken conventional management courses.

They have been taught that the boss's job is to "plan," "lead," "organize," "control," and "coordinate" the work of others, and they're convinced that the reason why they're in the shape they're in is because I, their manager, have failed to plan, lead, organize, control, and coordinate their work. No wonder their morale is up when they see me finally doing what they were taught I am paid to do.

I can remember many years ago my first job as an hourly worker in one of our local factories. I can recall many a Saturday morning when I and my buddies were in the plant getting caught up. We knew that our bosses were on the golf course. That was how we workers thought it should be because that was how the "incentive system" worked back in those days. But here it is years later; I'm still in the office. A whole new generation is on the golf course, and I muse, "My gosh, when did the incentive system pass me by?"

The Revelation

Well, at that point the clouds part and I get the revelation as clearly as Moses atop Mt. Sinai. And I say:

"I see it now. They're not working for me; I'm working for them!"

It dawns on me that their frustration results from the fact that they have surrendered to me all their initiatives, and that my guilt results from the fact that I'm never going to get caught up.

My problem has its roots in an old psychological principle, attributed to B. F. Skinner, that goes this way: "Any form of behavior that you reward you will reinforce."

It suddenly dawns on me that if I do any of the things I came to the office to do this weekend, I would only make matters worse. Why?

- If I reward George for bringing me his problems by solving them for him, the frequency and the difficulty of the problems he brings me to solve in the future will only go up.

- If I reward Mike for sending me weekly progress reports by reading them and answering them on time and with precision, the difficulty and the length of the progress reports I get from him in the future will only increase.

In short, if I do any of the things I came to do, I will only run the input up to a much faster rate than my output. I am only one person limited by 24 hours a day, but four people are feeding me stuff, and they're working under capacity right now. One "employee" cannot work for four "managers" who are spending all their time thinking up things for the one to do!

If you're a hard-working person taking orders from four "skilled," "imaginative" executives, you're headed for disaster. In other words . . .

The more you do, the more you will get to do.

Because practice makes perfect, eventually I will develop a group of people who are the best question askers anywhere. Then, if I should drop dead, the company will have lost the one man with all the answers, and it will have to turn my department over to the people with all the questions. Wish that catastrophe on your competitors!

I now have the revelation indelibly written in my consciousness:

The more I get caught up, the more I will fall behind.

This statement of the problem happens to apply only to management work. It is not true of vocational and professional work. In vocational and professional work, the more you get caught up, the more caught up you will be. That is why, as we move into management, we continue to feel that "getting caught up" is the answer to the problem, because it worked so well at the vocational and professional level.

For example, if you are in engineering, and you fall behind in your drawings, I would say, "Go to the office over the weekend and get caught up," and you will be. If you are in accounting, and you're behind in balancing the books, I would say, "Go to the office over the weekend and get caught up," and you will be. But if you're behind in management work, then the more you get caught up, the further behind you'll get.

I ask you, in whose work am I behind? If I took my briefcase to the police department, criminology lab, fingerprint section and asked them to tell me whose work this is by identifying the oldest fingerprints on each piece of paper, in whose work would they say I am behind? My subordinates' work. I haven't been behind in my work for 15 years! I haven't had the time to get it started, preoccupied as I have been with my subordinates' monkeys!

Priorities for Discretionary Time

When I see that, I realize that out of all of the places I might be this weekend, it would be most disastrous to spend another second at the office. So I snap my briefcase shut with the precision of a man who has seen a vision and run down that hallway as fast as my legs will carry me.

The weekend janitor says, "Mr. Oncken, where are you going in such a hurry?" And I say, "Get out of my way. My speed is not explained by where I'm going; it's explained by where I'm leaving from."

I vault down those stairs, hitting every sixth step. I jump into the car, and I head in a random direction of the compass, and 10 minutes later I find myself on the outskirts of town. I don't know where I am; I don't know where I'm going. I have no plans for the weekend.

So then I look heavenward and say, "Dear Spirit, I don't know what to do with my discretionary time, not having had any for some 15 years. What do I do?"

She says, "Get caught up on something you can get caught up on—get caught up now on the rating that God is making of you everyday on your performance in the other roles you play in life, which presumably is what you get up for every morning. And you have got a lot of catching up to do."

I say, "Have you seen my most recent perform-ance evaluation? Do I have a chance?"

She says, "Yes, I looked at it this morning, and you do have a chance because it's still blank."

Encouraged by that evaluation, I make a U-turn and head for home to see if I can head my family off before they go their several ways that Saturday morning. I make it back in the nick of time, pull up in front of the house to a screeching halt, lean out my car window, and holler, "Hey, honey! Hey, kids! Pick up what you need. We're going on that picnic!" They know which picnic I'm talking about. It's a very special one—the picnic I haven't had time to go on for 15 years. Confused, they pile into the car.

Together we head down to the county play-ground where we knock ourselves out all day at badmitton, volleyball, shuffle board, and all of the other pleasures provided by the town council.

Sunday morning I go to church with my fami-ly. I can't remember the last time I went to church with the family on Sunday. That afternoon we head back to the playground, and in the evening I go to bed in perfect peace.

From Subordinate-Imposed to Discretionary Time

Let's cut the story right here and see what hap-pened. Here are my questions:

- When I arrived at the office that Saturday morning, I was committed to putting in two full days (60 monkeys x 30 minutes per monkey = 30 hours work) of which kind of time: subordinate-imposed or discretionary? Subordinate-imposed.

- It is now 15 minutes later. I have no plans for the weekend, don't know where I am, don't know where I'm going. I am now committed to two full days of which kind of time? Discretionary.

Changing two full days of subordinate-imposed time to two full days of discretionary time in the short space of 15 minutes is an act that cannot be pulled off by the will of the flesh. That requires divine intervention. By "the will of the flesh," I mean that it generally takes 15 years for people to wise up to this concept.

chapter seven

How to Keep Monkeys on the Proper Backs

Sunday night I go to bed and sleep soundly for 10 hours; in fact, I sleep so soundly that twice during the night my wife figures I am dead. On both occasions she puts a flashlight in my face to find out what is going on, and there she sees a beautiful, angelic smile all over my visage.

What am I smiling about? I'll tell you what I'm smiling about. I have very definite plans for George, Mike, Valerie, and Dave for Monday morning. That's what I'm smiling about. I've never gone to bed on a Sunday night with a clearer idea in my head as to what Monday morning was going to be like than I have now.

The Plan

Tomorrow I will prepare the ground for ridding myself of subordinate-imposed time by transferring the initiative from my back to the backs of my subordinates. In exchange, I will get an equal amount of discretionary time, part of which I will spend with my subordinates to see that they learn the difficult but rewarding managerial art called "The Care and Feeding of Monkeys." I will now, for the first time, be working *with* them rather than *for* them.

I will also have some discretionary time for getting control of the timing and content of my boss-imposed and system-imposed time.

The degree to which I gain this control depends on me and my skill in satisfying my boss and conforming to the demands of the system. My success depends on how well my boss, peers, and subordinates understand what I am doing. Otherwise, there can still be trouble on all fronts.

My reward will be additional discretionary time, which will enable me to do the creative, original, innovative thinking and strategic planning the company hired me to do. You cannot be creative and innovate without discretionary time to do it in, but you've got to get control of your staff environment before you'll ever get the discretionary time to pull this off—and that can take time.

Monday morning, after getting 10 hours of refreshing slumber, I go downstairs for breakfast, pick up my monkey cage, and head through the kitchen door to the garage with a spring in my step. I drive to work, whistling all the way.

I pull into the parking lot and enter the office building, eager to encounter the very people I avoided last week. As I approach my office, what do I see? A familiar sight: these four "crows" sitting, as it were, on a clothesline outside my office, poised to ask the same questions:

- "Oncken, what are we going to do about the budget overrun?"

- "Oncken, what are we going to do about the cost-cutting program?

- "We're behind. How are we supposed to make a progress report in a couple of days."

- "Oncken, what are we going to do about the problem we have with one of our key customers."

I avoided these people last week because I saw in them the source of all my problems.

But now, as I approach these people, I realize that what happened to me on Saturday morning was obviously a miraculous conversion because now I see them differently. How can anybody switch from hate to love in 48 hours? It had to be by divine intervention. Why do I love these people? Because for the first time in my life I see in each of them a potential repository for several monkeys. I imagine taking all the monkeys on my back, and spreading them out over five backs, thereby reducing the monkey density by 80 percent. (The number of monkeys per back is called "monkey density.")

I walk past them with a dead-pan expression, not revealing how I feel, but I'm a bad actor. They see inscribed in both my eyeballs a cheery good morning. That change in my behavior so throws them off balance that they simply stare in silence and disbelief as I walk past. Sue, my assistant, notices another change in my behavior—I do not shut my door. I haven't said a word yet. Nevertheless, everyone in the office can sense a dynamic change in the leadership climate.

Putting the Monkeys on the Proper Backs

I call them into my office, one by one. The purpose of each interview is to take a monkey, place it on the desk between us, and figure out together how the next move might be theirs.

For certain monkeys, this will take some doing. The next move may be so elusive that I may decide—just for now—merely to let the monkey sleep overnight on George's back and have him return with it at an appointed time the next morning to continue the joint quest for a more substantive move on his part.

Now, to be sure, it may turn out to be my monkey because, as we say, "Every monkey has a homeroom." It may be my monkey, no question about it. But if it is, where does the burden of proof lie? With him. And while he is proving to me that it's mine, where must that monkey lie? On his back. Then I can in rational, studied fashion pick the monkey up and put it on my back where it belongs. *But to heck with this business of pick-*

ing up monkeys by default! For if the monkey leaps on my back, and it turns out later to be really his, I can tell you from personal experience that to tear a monkey off your back to put it on a staff member's back where it really belongs is very painful. So rather than go through that agony, don't let the monkey leap at all until you determine whose monkey it is. If it is the subordinate's, then it's his or her next move.

Suppose some of the monkeys are mine, but I can't work on them right now. If I keep the monkeys that are decisions only I can make, what would I do with them? If your filing system resembles mine, it has no room for certain monkeys, such as odd-ball, one-shot things. In short, I might lose them if I hang onto them. But if I ask my subordinates to be custodians of something, then if they can't find it, they are guilty of insubordination. Therefore, the best way not to lose anything is not to file it—give it to your subordinates to file. Then, if they can't find it, they have a career problem. If you're smart, you'll have practically nothing at all in your office (it will all be out in the trenches with the troops).

For instance, picture a member of my staff bringing an issue to my attention, and it is obvious that the next move will be mine. I can say, "Well, I guess that monkey is mine. Only I can do it. You're not authorized to do it. But you can see, George, from the pile of work on my desk, that I'm not going to get to that thing in the next 24 hours. So for the next 24 hours, George, that monkey will have to sleep overnight some place. I suppose it will sleep just as soundly on your back as it will on mine. So please tend this thing, and be back tomorrow, 24 hours from now, for its feeding."

He goes out with the monkey on his back, but he won't do a thing with it, right? Of course not. It's my next move, but I'm not going to get to it. I figure if nothing will be done about a thing, better that nothing be not done in his briefcase than in mine.

He comes back the next day and says, "Here's your monkey." I say, "What shape's it in?" He says, "It's in the same shape as when I took it out yesterday." I say, "Well, you can look at my desk, and you know as well as I do I'm not going to get to it for another 24 hours. Please babysit it for another 24 hours and report back." He leaves and returns as requested the next day. I say, "What shape's it in?" "Same shape it was before." We keep doing this. After about the 35th round trip, nothing has yet been done. Keep in mind that nothing would have been done, either, had I kept the monkey.

Where would it have been if I'd kept it? In my "to do" file, staring at me, making me feel guiltier and guiltier. Instead, after the 35th round trip he gets sick and tired of this. So he says to me, "Look, Oncken, how long is this game going to last? I must get rid of this monkey. It's stuck to me like flypaper. How do I get rid of it?" I say, "I don't know, George, how you're going to get rid of the monkey." If I'd only given that monkey to George to file someplace, he wouldn't worry about it. It's the round trips that are getting to him. I say, "I don't know how you might get rid of this monkey, George, except one way. That would be if you would come up with an idea. I know that would be a novel experience for you, but don't hold back."

Now we've got the pleasure-pain principle working, right? He's got two unpleasant courses of action before him: one is to keep up an indefinite number of round trips, which would be painful; the other is to come up with an idea, which could also be painful. Which do you think he will regard as being slightly less painful? To come up with an idea. He could go around, pick other people's brains, find out I'm not the only resource in this company, test things out, try them out on other people, and finally come up with an idea that might astonish me.

George picks up the monkey, turns, and leaves my office. As he leaves, I see something I have not seen in years—George's back . . . with a monkey screwed squarely between his shoulder blades. So between now and our scheduled "monkey feeding appointment," I will be waiting for him, he will not be waiting for me.

Several times that afternoon, I walk by his office, stick my head in, and say, "Hi, George, how's it coming?"

I tell you, there's nothing like it! Of course, by the time he answers that question, I'm way down the hallway—I never hear the answer. I don't care about the answer now; I'll find out at monkey-feeding time. All I want is a chance to ask the question once in a while—a novel experience for me. It's called "job therapy for managers."

Developing Your Staff

Who has the monkey now? George does. Who has the initiative? George. Who has the control of the timing and content of the work? George. But who has more discretionary time? Ah, I do.

That's the way a professional manager develops his people. But George has a long way to go before he is really the self-reliant manager he always thought he wanted to be.

But all journeys, even those of a thousand miles, begin with a first step, a next move, an initiative, "a monkey."

If monkey management is a totally new experience for George, then he might begin to show symptoms of "distress." He may be plagued with nervous twitches, gas pains, or brain cramps. He believes he needs help with this monkey and will come to me, his boss, for that help. Often when a subordinate comes to the boss for help, he is not looking for a solution but rather for a solver!

So I say to George, "I want to be of all the help to you I can. It's my job to help you, and I've got all the time to do it. However, to help you, we've got to have an understanding, first, as to what the situation is, and second, what the ground rule is. When we understand that, I can be of help to you. First, the situation. Tell me, George, is this problem your problem or my problem?"

George says, "Well, Oncken, as I recall we set it up as being my problem."

I say, "That's right. Therefore, here comes the ground rule:

At no time while I'm helping you with your problem will your problem become my problem.

"Because the instant your problem becomes my problem, you will no longer have a problem, and I cannot help a man who hasn't got a problem. And I want to help you.

"So when this meeting is over, the problem will leave this office exactly the way it came in—on your back." This is an illustration of a basic principle of physics: when output equals input, there's no accumulation.

"You may ask my help at any appointed time, and we will make a joint determination of what the next move will be and which of us will make it.

"In those rare instances where the next move turns out to be mine, you and I will determine it together, and I will not make any move alone. Ground rule accepted, George?"

He says, "Yes."

I say, "By the way, when will you make the next move?"

He says, "Well, I can talk to Accounting this afternoon."

"When can you be back in my office with your decision?"

He says, "Tomorrow at 9 a.m." He gets up and walks out. The monkey is on his back; the date's on my calendar pad. For the next 24 hours I will be waiting for him, he will not be waiting for me.

I'm sure you know why I'm putting that appointment on my calendar pad. It is not for coercive purposes, but to enable him to know the precise time tomorrow after which he will be insubordinate if he either 1) doesn't show up or 2) shows up with nothing. Again, it is reasonable to require that a person show up, and to require that he show up with something.

Reviews are scheduled to eliminate the possibility of procrastination. Why? Because subordinates will RESPECT what you INSPECT, but not everything you EXPECT. Procrastination is invited when there are no established monkey-feeding appointments. One cannot be late when there is no date, and if there is no possibility of being late (and, therefore, no penalty), pressure to act is reduced. For the good of everyone concerned, schedule progress reviews. They are enormously helpful in maintaining the health of monkeys.

Creating Good Mental Health

Feeling like a young dentist who just successfully pulled his first tooth, I yell, "Next." And I take each of my subordinates in rapid succession. By 10:30 in the morning I've got all these monkeys right back where they came from.

As a result of my conversion to a professional manager:

- I no longer have my subordinates' monkeys,

- the four chairs outside my office are now empty,

- I am no longer holding up my subordinates,

- I am no longer a source of their frustration, and

- I no longer feel guilty.

Anything you do to reduce the level of frustration and guilt in an organization is the road to mental health for everybody. While this is a leap forward, it doesn't mean they're happy. They're just mentally more healthy.

But right now, down the hallway, they are griping over the fact that they are overworked. They are not, of course, but because everything is relative, compared to the nothing they've been doing, anything is overwork by comparison. They're calling me all kinds of names: "Goof-Off Oncken," "Cop-Out Oncken," "Dump-the-Work Oncken." They're commiserating with each other, as suddenly I have become a top-down, heavy-handed, autocratic ogre.

Even though they may think they are overworked, what really happened? They swapped their frustration for feelings of being overworked. But what is it that really kills people? Overwork or frustration? Frustration always kills! Overwork never does. You can't kill a person through overwork. If you want to kill people, the fastest way to do it is to grab their monkeys and lock them up in your safe. Don't let them get their fingers on these monkeys, and within three months, they'll be climbing the walls. Frustration kills.

So these chairs outside my office are now empty at 11:30 this morning. And we're on our way to mental health even though we've got to put up with a certain amount of complaining and belly-aching. But that's normal and to be expected.

Transferring the Initiative

The point of our monkey-on-the-back analogy is to transfer the initiative from managers to subordinates and keep it there. But before managers can develop initiative in people, they must see to it that the staff members have the initiative. Once managers take back the initiative, their staffs will no longer have it, and they can kiss their discretionary time goodbye. It will all revert to subordinate-imposed time.

Both manager and subordinate cannot effectively have the same initiative at the same time. The opener, "Boss, we've got a problem," implies this duality and represents, as noted earlier, a monkey astride two backs, which is a very bad way to start a monkey on its career.

Well, if those are the key differences between subordinate-imposed and discretionary time, it should be a relatively easy matter to get a good slice of the discretionary time you need. All you have to do is keep the monkey where it belongs—on your subordinate's back.

chapter eight

Monkeys + Freedom = Empowerment

The **Oncken Freedom Scale** articulates five levels of initiative subordinates can exercise in relation to their boss:

(5) **act** on own, then routinely report (highest initiative);

(4) **act,** but advise "at once" (which is anything more frequent than "routine");

(3) **recommend,** then take resulting action;

(2) **ask** what to do;

(1) **wait** until told (lowest initiative).

The Manager's Goal

Clearly, anyone should be professional enough not to operate on Freedom Levels 1 and 2 in relation to their boss, and no manager should permit staff members to operate there either. Managers who use Level 1 have no control over both the timing and the content of their job, thereby forfeiting any right to complain about what they are told to do or when they are told to do it. Managers who use Level 2 have some control over the timing, but no control over the content. Levels 3, 4, and 5 leave managers in control of both, with the greatest control being at Freedom Level 5.

If we could ask the late Dr. Abraham Maslow—the prominent management consultant who came up with the hierarchy of human needs—where on the **Oncken Freedom Scale** one would mostly likely be able to self-actualize, I'm sure he would tell us, "Toward the top."

And yet for 15 years my subordinates operated at Freedom Levels 1 and 2—moving directly opposite their self-actualization and the organization's best interests. Why? Because I had rewarded that kind of behavior, and, as B. F. Skinner once noted, any behavior you reward you will reinforce.

What we want in our organizations are self-reliant, rather than boss-reliant, people, who can seize the initiative—take the necessary action to get things done. The word "act" appears only at Freedom Levels 3 and above. Our goal as managers is two-fold:

- To outlaw the use of both Freedom Levels 1 and 2 by our direct reports, thus giving subordinates no choice but to master the twin arts of formulating and "selling" their ideas and recommendations.

- To see that for each task (monkey) leaving our office on a subordinate's back there is an agreed-upon level of freedom and an agreed-upon time and place of our next manager-managee conference. The latter should be duly noted on our—the manager's—appointment calendar to ensure that the monkey does not eventually starve to death (a victim of procrastination).

How does a professional manager go about outlawing initiatives at Levels 1 and 2 without disrupting the entire organization?

Outlawing Freedom Level 1

How do you get people out of the habit of "waiting for you to tell them what to do?"

The principal tool is the "job description." Of course, job descriptions turn many people off because they've had bad experiences with them. But razors also turn many people off, too, because they've had bad experiences with them.

The real purpose of a job description is to *spell out the duties and responsibilities about which the individual has no authority to simply do nothing.* A job description typically lists broad general duties, responsibilities, roles, and functions. If managers have not done anything about one of those items, they have already exceeded their authority because they didn't have the authority to simply do nothing about it. A decision to do nothing is just as significant as a decision to do something. If they do not have the authority to make the decision to do nothing, they have nothing left to do but do something.

For example, suppose that Mike works for me, and we go over his job description to ensure that it is current and up to date. I ask him what he has going in item No. 1, and he tells me. Item No. 2, and he tells me. When he gets to item No. 3, I say, "What have you got going there, Mike?"

He says, "I'm spending a lot of time on that."

I say, "I'm sure you are, Mike. However, can you produce some 'footprints in the sands of time' that say something went by this way recently? Please don't get me wrong, Mike. I'm not trying to evaluate your performance; I'm only trying to locate it!"

Have you any idea how many managers are trying to evaluate performance that does not even exist? Unless the boss can see it, it plainly is not happening.

Outlawing Freedom Level 2
How do you get people out of the habit of "asking you what to do?"

If subordinates ask you what to do in certain areas of their job responsibilities, the logical inference is that they are currently doing nothing. To do nothing when required to do something is, by definition, insubordination. Again, we want our staff people to take the initiative, take the necessary action to get things done. The word "act" appears only at Freedom Levels 3 and above.

I suggest that in the margin opposite each responsibility listed in their job descriptions, you spell out what authority (or Freedom Level) your people have to carry it out. Assign each job responsibility a number 3, 4, or 5. What determines the level of their authority? Your own anxiety—concerning the issue and your confidence (or lack of it) in your subordinate's abilities to successfully discharge that responsibility—is the only thing that determines that level of authority.

When your people have their job description appended with nothing but 5s, 4s, and 3s, then when one of them then comes to you and says, "Boss, what do you want me to do?", you can smile and say, "Is the question you're asking me related to some area of your job description?" "Yeah," your staffer says, "Come to think of it, it's item nine of my responsibilities." You then require that they come back to you at least with a recommendation wrapped in marketable form, taking into full account your buying habits.

Frequently people ask me, "Bill, how do you get people to take the initiative?" I reply, "Remove all other alternatives!"

Coaching People Up the Freedom Scale

If you expect people to become self-reliant members of an interdependent team, don't do their jobs for them! When your subordinates come to you for help, often they are not looking for help. What they are looking for is to get your fingerprints on their murder weapon. Any rifle coach will tell you that if you want to develop a winning rifle team, do everything you can to help your team members, but keep you fingers off their triggers. Because if you pull their triggers for them, whose skill in marksmanship will you be improving—yours or theirs? Yours. Whose skill in marksmanship are you being paid to improve? Theirs. So give all the help you can, but keep your hands off their weapons. They will eventually realize that help is not all it's cracked up to be. Then later, when they run into a problem, they'll realize they can spend their time more profitably in target practice than tying up their valuable hours in your office trying to deal with an inferior mind.

Freedom Levels 4 and 5 are an earned privilege—they are neither an entitlement nor a right. Such privileges are earned by developing a reputation of being able to sell one's ideas and recommendations to one's boss. This reputation can only be developed at Freedom Level 3.

Suppose that one of your subordinates is beginning his journey at Freedom Level 3. When anything comes up in that part of his job, he comes to you and says, "Boss, here's the problem. There are three possible courses of action to take care of it." He describes them "A, B, and C." He then tells you, "Here are the pros and cons of A, here are the pros and cons of B, and here are the pros and cons of C. I believe it would be to your best advantage if I pursued alternative C." What is he trying to do?

He's trying to get you to buy, right? He's trying to get you to back his recommendation. This puts him in what role? Salesman. We hope his product is sound, but having a sound recommendation is not enough—you must not only be right, but your recommendation must be bought and backed by higher management. Until it is, you have accomplished nothing.

What is any product or service in the world worth until somebody buys it? Nothing. It happens to be the function of the marketplace to determine what something is worth in our free-enterprise economy. Products, therefore, have no intrinsic worth, nor do management ideas have any intrinsic worth. So when managers say to me "Bill, I have a dozen dynamite ideas, but do you think those stupid guys in the front office know a good idea when they see one? Hell no. They're backward, narrow-minded, stuck in their traditional ways of thinking." I ask you, what is the real value of his ideas? Nothing. "Let the customer be the judge of the feast, not the chef." If he is successful in selling me (his boss) on the idea, then he'll take the action that results from our dialogue, and he will use the best skill in salesmanship available to him appropriate to the situation.

Completed Staff Work

The very best in salesmanship skills is embodied in the military's concept of "Completed Staff Work"—where you don't let your boss get anything until it's at the point where he's ready to decide whether it's "go" or "no go."

Of course, in the ideal world, the work ought to be done so completely on paper that the boss, just reading it, can say yes or no. But that does not take into account the emotional factor. Completed Staff Work should include sufficient dialogue so that the boss can relax over it. He now has sufficient confidence in his subordinate's competence, rapport with his personality, respect for his character, *and* a terrific proposal. All of that goes together in the boss's consciousness, and the subordinate earns the privilege to act.

My father applied these same coaching principles in our home. I recall that back in high school I ran into something in mathematics called quadratic equations. I went to my mother for help because, in addition to having once taught summer school algebra, she would give me the kind of help I wanted. I would say to her, "Mother, how do you solve this problem?" She said, "I'll show you how to solve it." So she solved it for me. So I then said, "Mother, how do you solve this one?" She said, "I'll show you how to solve it." So she solved it. She did that for 10 problems. I took all of her 'show-hows' and copied it in my own handwriting, went to school, and got 100. I came back and said to my father, "Dad, I got 100." He said, "No, your mother did." At the time I didn't understand what he was talking about because I thought I got 100 with my mother's help. Well, after my mother finally got fed up with my daily implorings, she said, "Look, your dad taught advanced mathematics for four years. He knows a lot more about this than I do. Go to him for help."

When I went to my father for help, he said, "Bill, I'd be thrilled to help you, but I've lost the skill of answering questions. However, I became enormously skilled at asking them. So you'll have to labor with this handicap I have. I can only ask, I cannot answer. So the way we're going to divide the labor is this: I'm asking the questions, and you're answering them. Now, what can I do for you?"

I said, "How do you solve this problem?"

Dad replied, "Wait a minute. I'm asking the questions. When will you be back with your best efforts at solving this problem?"

I answered, "Well, how about 30 minutes?"

So Dad said, "That's fine."

In half an hour I came back and showed him what I had. Dad opined, "That'll never do. That's wrong."

I said, "What's wrong with it?"

He said, "That's for you to find out."

I came back the next time. Dad looked at it and said, "Wrong again." I knew better than to ask him what's wrong with it because he was asking the questions, I was answering them. On about the ninth runaround, I showed Dad what I had. It was right, but it took me an hour and a half. The next problem took me another hour, and by midnight I only had three problems done out of 10. So I went to my mother and said, "Mother, please help me with my problems."

She said, "I told you to go to your father. He knows a lot more about it than I do."

I said, "I know he does, but I don't want to learn that much about it."

The same thing can happen to our staff members, and that's why they may appear nervous as we work them up their Freedom Scales. The purpose of coaching is to develop self-reliance in our subordinates. Self-reliance is an acquired trait requiring self-discipline, patience, and persistence on everyone's part.

chapter nine

Six Rules for the Care and Feeding of Monkeys and Gorillas

Once you entrust a monkey to someone, and both of you know what degree of freedom he or she will enjoy with regard to the monkey, and what degree of protection from potential staff mistakes you will enjoy, you still need to administer further preventive treatment in the interest of the monkey's health. The fact that the monkey is insured and that the person has a specified freedom of action is usually sufficient to keep the monkey alive, but insufficient to ensure that the monkey will flourish.

Accordingly, I will now prescribe a course of action I call **The Six Rules for the Care and Feeding of Monkeys and Gorillas**.

103

Monkey-feeding time is simply that time spent in dialogue when you ask a person, "How's it coming?" with regard to a particular monkey, and he or she answers your question. You may ask that question many times during the lifetime of a monkey or gorilla, depending how anxious you are about it. Feeding time may last only a couple of minutes in the case of a small monkey (assignment), or it may take hours to feed a big gorilla (project). Feeding rules are the same for both monkeys and gorillas; however, projects require more dialogue because they are more complex.

The First Two Rules

Rule 1: *Feed them or shoot them, but do not let them starve to death.*

Rule 2: *Your subordinates will find time to work as many monkeys and gorillas as you find them to feed, but no more.*

The first two rules can be best illustrated with the story of a friend I will call Jack. At the time I knew him, he lived and worked in Chicago, where he was executive vice president of a company employing about 2,500 people. He had been hired to turn that company around in two years. In other words, he was a downsizer, a "hatchet man"!

I first met Jack when he was in the middle of his two-year term. He retained me to do some consulting work, to come in the first three days of every month, make studies, write a report, leave, and then repeat the same process every month.

Rule 1

Make sure your monkeys and gorillas don't starve to death!

A Top Management Revolt

On one occasion when I showed up, Jack was waiting for me in the lobby. He whisked me off to his office, shut the door, and in hushed tones confided in me a problem that he wanted me to tackle. He said, "Bill, I have a serious problem with Bob."

Bob was Jack's vice president in charge of Research and Development. He was a young fellow, 35 years old, with a master's degree in mechanical engineering from MIT, and he managed six other people in Research and Development.

"In the year I've been here, Bob has grown increasingly uncooperative. This is a serious handicap to me, especially since Bob is not alone. He has a charismatic quality about him, and the other vice presidents are following his lead. What I have is a strike at the top management level, and we must break this thing up! The only way I know to do it is to get Bob back into the fold, and then the other vice presidents will follow him."

"What do you want me to do?" I asked.

"I see from your schedule," Jack said, "that you're having lunch with Bob today. During lunch, will you please explore that man's mind for me and then report back to me?"

Well, I'm no psychiatrist, and I shouldn't have accepted that assignment, but I agreed to do it anyway.

Later that day, Bob and I went to lunch together, and I shared with him the problem that was Jack's concern. When I had finished, Bob was thoughtfully silent for a moment. He then said, "Jack is right. I have not been cooperating with him in the past, and I don't see any reason to cooperate in the future!"

"Boy!" I said. "That's a bold admission. What's up?"

"Well, Oncken, Jack brings the whole thing on himself. You know that Jack is a brilliant man. He has an IQ of 160, got his bachelor's degree when he was 16, his MBA when he was 18, came to Chicago and had a rocket-like rise in the company. And because he has such a brilliant mind and is so enormously creative, he does things that drive me and my staff to distraction.

"Every morning he comes to work a half hour early, dives into his email, and devours all the reports on yesterday's sales and operations. He has a computer in his head, and he can memorize those numbers rapidly. He then makes a series of guerrilla raids on the office. He'll walk down the hall, see Joe, and say, 'When you get a chance, see if you can come up with a layout that'll solve that safety hazard in Building 3.'

"Jack walks into another office, sees Henry, and says, 'We need to reduce overhead. The Personnel Department told me just yesterday that four union machinists will retire next month, so we could accomplish this reduction with attrition rather than moving people around. When you get a chance, see which course would be most effective.'

"Jack keeps generating ideas and walking around the place, dropping an idea on one guy here and another idea on that guy. And the recipients are all saying 'I'll get right on it, Jack. Get right on it. Don't worry about it. I'll take care of it.' And that is how it goes!"

"How about you, Bob?" I said. "Does Jack drop any of his ideas on you?"

"He certainly does. And Jack would never believe it, but I do take these things seriously. I pick up about seven of these assignments a week from Jack, at random times, in random places. Every Friday night I sit down, and I add the ones I got that week to a list I keep on my computer—28 of them on this list. Every Friday evening before I quit for the week, I take the seven I just got from him this week, add them to the head of this list, and drop the bottom seven off in order to keep the list from getting over 28, because I think 28 is about all a person can handle.

"The following week I take the seven I got from him that week, add them to the top of the list, drop the bottom seven off to keep it from getting over 28. That means this list turns over 100 percent every four weeks. So what happens when I try to work on one of the items, say the top one on the list? Before I can get my hands on it, the darned thing has slithered down the page, off the bottom, and into the trash can. That is what has been happening, and that is why I am not cooperating with Jack."

I gazed at Bob with speechless astonishment. Finally, I said, "Why don't you just take a pencil, close your eyes, and poke that pencil into that list of items you have there. Poke it anywhere at random, select an item, and work on that one. Even if it falls off the bottom, stay with it. Give the man something!"

"I'll be glad to do that, Oncken," said Bob, "if you will just take this list back to Jack and ask him to go through it and first cross off all of those items he has by now long since forgotten about, and then to go through the list a second time and cross off all those items he no longer cares about. Bring me back the list and I will be happy to work on the three that are left. Three out of 28 is roughly 10 percent. That means that if I work on some item that I hit at random, the chances are nine out of 10 that I'll be wasting my time, and I'm too busy to work against odds like that."

I said, "Bob, you have explained the nature of the problem brilliantly. I can't wait to tell Jack what it is!"

Revelation and Confession, But No Reform

When I returned to Jack's office later that afternoon, he asked me immediately, "Did you have lunch with Bob?"

"Yes, I did."

"Did he tell you what the problem is?"

"Yes, he did, with crystal clarity!"

"What is it?"

"Jack, you're going to need a shock absorber before you get the statement of the problem." So we went around the corner into the cocktail lounge. After Jack had had two double martinis and was in the proper spiritual frame of mind to receive the revelation, I gave it to him.

When I finished describing the problem, Jack's reaction surprised me. He turned red in the face, and, feeling guilty, quoted Bobby Burns: "Would that God give us the gift to see ourselves as others see us."

"It is criminal," he said, "for anybody to treat people like that. I never realized I was doing it . . . this is awful!"

At that point, I began to get an uneasy feeling because I was playing the role of somebody listening to a confessional, and this does not happen to be one of my vocational skills. So to get out of this uneasy situation, I reached across the table and said, "Jack, get hold of yourself, man. It isn't as bad as all that. After all, you are not the world's worst amateur. The world's worst amateur is the compulsive monkey-picker-upper, and that's not you. You're only the second worst amateur. You are the prolific monkey-dropper. You drop them by the thousands every day!" I had temporarily forgotten that Jack knew nothing about "monkeys."

"Oncken, I may have had a couple of martinis, but that does not explain the fact that I don't understand your vocabulary!"

"My apologies" I said, and I then gave him an abbreviated explanation of the concept of monkeys and next moves.

Rule 2

Determine your optimum monkey/gorilla population.

"What I recommend, Jack, is that you keep right on doing what you're doing. There are thousands of managers who will never learn how to drop monkeys, but somehow you have mastered that skill. So hang on to it. However, I would recommend that you do something more. You see, Jack, your problem is that you don't realize that unless monkeys are put on feeding schedules, they will starve to death. That odor you are complaining to me about is from the rotting carcasses of monkeys that are starving to death for lack of feeding.

"Keep on dropping monkeys as you have been, but before you leave a man with his last words being, 'I'll get right on it, Jack,' reach for your appointment calendar, open it up, and say, 'When can you be in my office to spend no more than five minutes answering a very simple question, 'How's it coming?'

"When the two of you come to an agreement, write on your calendar something like this: 'Thursday, from 2:00 to 2:05, feed John Smith's monkey No. 9.' You see, Jack you have an inventory. Every monkey will have an inventory symbol in two parts. The first part will be the name of the person on whose back the monkey is, and the second part will be the serial number, right? Then all monkeys will be inventoried; none of them ever get lost; they will never starve to death because they will be fed—each one at an appointed time. Jack, look what this means. Five minutes to feed one monkey; in an hour you can feed 12; in a day you can feed 96 monkeys. None of them will die, and there won't be any more stink."

"It'll never work," said Jack.

"Why?"

"Because I drop millions of monkeys every day, and I don't have time to listen to all that crap!"

Well, I was crestfallen. I paid the tab; the two of us walked silently out. I took a cab to O'Hare Airport to go home, commiserating with myself for the lot of the management consultant who casts pearls before swine, who trample them under foot not realizing their value. Not only that, they pay for pearls they never use.

Finally, The Reformation

But one month later, I returned. This time I had lunch with another vice president who had no knowledge of my session with either Jack or Bob the previous month.

During lunch he said to me, "Oncken, something strange happened shortly after you left last month. Jack called a special meeting of all of us vice presidents, and he said, 'People, I've called this staff meeting because, after one year, it has now come to my attention that I have been attempting to do something as Executive Vice President of this company that the head of the monkey house at the Municipal Zoo would never think of doing.

"We have so many monkeys that we don't know how many there are, where they are, or how much fodder to order for them. We have a menagerie crawling with millions of monkeys, and many of them are dying and stinking up the place because they are not fed regularly. The monkey house at the zoo stinks, but not from rotting carcasses. So we must do what they do at the zoo; we are going to get ourselves an inventory of all the monkeys we have. Then we are going to decide which ones we can feed, and after that, we will divest ourselves of the surplus monkeys.'"

And then my friend said to me, "By the time Jack got to that point, we were all looking at each other, because we had all been praying for his death, but as we heard what Jack was saying, we realized that God answers prayers in the strangest ways. Raving insanity is a viable alternative to death, so we thought we'd just sit there and let the guy hang himself.

"But then Jack explained to us what he meant by the term 'monkey,' and continued, saying, 'So what we will do first is inventory the monkeys. Then, because we have too many to feed, we will assassinate monkeys until we get the population down to a size we can feed. I want each of you to give me a list of everything you can recall that I ever asked you to do. Then you will come in one by one, and we'll go over your list, deciding which monkeys can be shot. Then the ones that are left will be put on feeding schedules."

Feed Some, Shoot the Others

My friend said that when he went into Jack's office, he had three pages of this stuff, and the two of them went over it together. And he said it was interesting because Jack realized that for every monkey that lived, he would have to find five minutes to feed it. He would have to sit down for five minutes and listen to the answer to the question, "How's it coming?" And Jack only had 40 or 50 hours in a week, and that was going to be the limit on how many monkeys he could have in his menagerie.

As they went down the list, they put "S" opposite some, meaning "shoot," and "F" opposite others, meaning "feed."

"As we went down that list, Jack said, 'We're going to shoot that one. Feed that one. Shoot that. That one we have to feed; it gets an "F" by it. Oh, my God, is this one still living? Blast its brains out. This one here we shoot. That we feed. That we shoot.'

"Sometimes we agonized over the decision to shoot a monkey, but we knew that there were some monkeys which had no relationship at all to the benefit of shareholders, customers, or our employees and their families. And if a monkey has nothing to do with those four, then it is merely a pet."

"Well," he said, "something like three-quarters of these monkeys came to a violent death. And on every one that had an "F" by it, Jack said, 'All right now, with regard to this monkey, when can you be in my office and spend no more time than five minutes telling me how it's coming?'

"Of course," said my friend, "of the monkeys that survived, some of them I didn't care for at all; I hated them and didn't want to work on them. Naturally, for those monkeys, I proposed a distant date. I would say to Jack, 'How about my reporting on this one 30 days from now?' But if Jack was anxious about that monkey, he would reply,

'No. That will not be acceptable. Instead, it will be 8 o'clock tomorrow morning when we talk.'"

New Priority Scheme

"When my boss said that," said my friend, "that changed my priorities in a way the priority systems we had been using had never changed them before. We used to sit in his office stacking priorities: top priority for this, next priority for that, next priority for that. That's an academic exercise in abstractions, because once we had that done, two days later the 'fit hit the shan,' and the whole place was now in shambles because by then everything was top priority. But there was no ambiguity when the boss said, 'I want to hear about it at 8 a.m., right?' That told me I had my day's work cut out for me.

"Priorities never again have had ambiguities because we watch to see how soon Jack wants to hear about it. Those things he's nervous about he wants to hear about right now, and those things he is not nervous about he doesn't want to hear about right now. This has clarified a lot of things!"

But I was curious about the drastic surgery performed on the monkey population. So I asked my friend, "Mass assassination is pretty severe action. Did you happen to shoot any of the wrong monkeys?"

"Oh," he said, "we probably did. But that's no problem at all."

"It isn't?"

"Certainly not. If you shoot the wrong monkey at 10 a.m., by quitting time the same day there will be four more monkeys applying for its job. So if you must make a mistake and shoot either too many or too few, always shoot too many!"

"Why?" I asked.

"In the interest of the ones that are still alive!" he replied with a knowing smile.

This brings us to a restatement of the first two rules for *The Care and Feeding of Monkeys:*

Rule 1: *Feed them or shoot them, but do not let them starve to death.*

Rule 2: *Your subordinates will find time to work as many monkeys and gorillas as you find them to feed, but no more.*

We know these rules intuitively. There is an old saying that "your people will respect only what you inspect, but not all that you expect." There are not enough hours in the day for any staff member to respect everything their boss expects, so the subordinates have to assign some kind of priorities. How do they do that? They do it the same way you do. If, on a Monday morning, you have two piles of monkeys on your desk, one pile with specific dates for taking action, the other pile with no dates, which gets your attention first? The pile with the dates, of course. If your subordinates are going to procrastinate something, they'll delay those items which are to be acted on "when convenient" or "as soon as possible."

So do yourself and your subordinates a favor. The next time you give one of them a monkey, negotiate a date when the two of you will meet to ask and answer the question, "How's it coming?" The date need not be the completion date of the assignment or project; indeed, depending upon how anxious you are about the monkey, the two of you may meet many times during the course of the assignment or project. Bosses put their time where their anxieties are, not where their brains are, and chances are that the things you are most anxious about, your subordinates will be most anxious about.

The way to communicate your anxieties and priorities is by using monkey-feeding appointments. If your anxieties are increasing (for whatever reason), increase the frequency of feeding times and decrease the intervals between feeding times. Your message will come through.

On the other hand, if you cannot find five minutes a week, or five minutes a month, to feed a monkey, your subordinates will conclude that if they must procrastinate something, the safest monkeys to procrastinate are those in which you have the least interest, and this must be one of them. When you run out of time for feeding monkeys, your subordinates run out of time for working them!

The Third Rule

Monkeys shall be fed on the the responsibility of the subordinate, at the time and place specified in the feeding schedule; bosses shall not be chasing down starving monkeys and feeding them on the fly, catch-as-catch-can.

Rule 3

The burden for feeding monkeys and gorillas must fall to the subordinate.

Conventional management training drums into our heads that one duty of managers is follow-up, follow-up, follow-up. What image does that conjure up in your mind? Chaser and chasee, right? The boss is the chaser, and the staff member is the chasee. This is not follow-up, it is harassment, and it can have ghastly consequences.

The Saga of an Amateur
Management By Wandering Around

In this scene, I, playing the role of Manager, come to work one day at 8 a.m., and by 10 a.m. I have completed most of the routine things and handled a few crises. I begin to get the funny feeling that I always get at 10 a.m. every morning—my people are probably dropping the ball *again*. So I get up from my desk and walk around to see if I can find what particular method they have chosen to use today. As I walk around the place, I remember what Benjamin Franklin's grandfather once observed: "When trouble is what you are looking for, you will be handsomely rewarded."

Sure enough, as I march down the hallway, I encounter Ed. He is a first-line supervisor in charge of Shipping and Receiving. He was appointed to that job out of the hourly ranks six months ago, and he is trying to do the job as he sees it.

He reports to a foreman, who in turn reports to a superintendent, who in turn reports to me. Ed and I are thus several supervisory levels removed from each other. As I look past Ed into the Shipping and Receiving Room, I see a crate. It is now 10:30 a.m. Thursday. That same crate was there last Monday.

The Amateur Feeds the Monkey

At once I jump on Ed. After all, he is the Shipping and Receiving Manager, right? He's right there, available. I confront him and say, "For goodness sake, Ed, you know I believe in human relations, sweetness and light, and a fine spirit which encourages creativity in the assumption of responsibility. But why don't we ship something around here once in a while?

"Last Monday I walked past that shipping dock, and I saw that crate there. I noticed it was consigned to one of our most valued customers, and I said to myself, 'Look at that, my team got that thing out here on the dock within hours after it came off the production line!' That made me feel great. Later that afternoon, though, it was still there. I wondered why it hadn't been shipped yet. Then again on Tuesday and Wednesday I saw it, and I suddenly got an attack of gas pains, heartburn, ulcers, and nervous twitches. Now, here it still is on Thursday!

"Ed, maybe you're not aware that the only way you get paid is if the customer gets delivery. That way we can invoice him and he pays us, right? So let's get that crate shipped!"

When I, the plant manager, ran into a monkey that was almost dead of starvation, I grabbed the little creature in one hand, force-fed it, flexed its little muscles, nursed it back to life and vigor, and handed it back to Ed. The scene ended as I went off in search of another starving monkey.

Here We Go Again!

Next I encounter Art in the Accounting Department. I say to him, "Art, you're an old-timer around here. You and I helped our founder put this company together with our bare hands. You know I don't go looking around for trouble. But, Art, look at those invoices, 60 days old. I know what the policy of your department is—to get invoices out within 30 days—so please spare me your excuses. All I want is a little evidence of that loyalty and devotion to duty that our president talked about in his annual Christmas message."

What happened? I found another monkey, almost dead of starvation. I grabbed the little thing, force-fed it, flexed its little muscles, nursed it back to life and vigor, handed it back to him, and ran off in search of another one.

What do managers who do this every day call this kind of activity? They call it supervision, checking up, or follow-up. It isn't any of these things—it's behaving like the warden of an insane asylum, driving the inmates crazier than the day they qualified for admission.

There Is More

But the worst is yet to come. That night, I, the plant manager, went home after everybody else had left (they are all constantly running out of work, while I am always running out of time). At home, after a big steak dinner, four cans of beer, and two TV shows, I poured myself exhausted into bed. But I could not get to sleep because I was kept up all night tormented by all the monkeys that got away that day. Having no inventory, I didn't know if I got 10 percent of them or 30 percent, and I was worried about all those that got away. So the next morning I went back to the plant and went through it in double time to get those monkeys I must have missed yesterday, plus the ones that needed feeding that day.

Wednesday I went through the plant triple time to catch the monkeys I should have got on Monday, plus those I missed on Tuesday, plus those I have to feed on Wednesday. And this goes on in an ever-spiraling crescendo, until on the 24th of the month, regularly, I call in sick. This is my monthly nervous breakdown. I have collapsed. I am out now for an entire week. This happens so regularly that the staffs plan on it. On their wall calendars they circle the 24th—that's the day that the old man loses his marbles. They use the week that I'm out under therapy to lock arm in arm and get caught up for all the time they lost when I was on the job! Restating this rule:

Rule 3: *Monkeys shall be fed on the the responsibility of the subordinate, at the time and place specified in the feeding schedule; bosses shall not be chasing down starving monkeys and feeding them on the fly, catch-as-catch-can.*

The first part suggests that if anybody's shoe leather is to be worn out feeding monkeys, it will be the subordinate's shoe leather. This means that subordinates shall come to the boss's office for monkey feeding; bosses shall not chase down starving monkeys. It can make subordinates nervous, and they can't do their best work under those circumstances.

Inspection Tours

If you are a manager, you should, of course, make excursions around the plant. Why? Because you are responsible for everything that goes on, whether you are there or not. Managers are as responsible for what goes on when they're in bed at three o'clock in the morning as they are responsible for what goes on when they are right there on the job. Because of that responsibility, you have to inform yourself, and one way of doing that is by practicing ubiquity.

"Ubi" in Latin means "everywhere." Ubiquity means the practice of "everywhereness." You have to get around, and if you don't think you can be everywhere at once, I will show you how to pull it off. I am going to replay this little skit, but this time, I will play it as a pro.

The Saga of a Professional
Management By Wandering Around

The Pro Feeds a Gorilla

When I get to work and look at my appointment calendar, I see that I'm scheduled to feed six monkeys today. Four of them I'll feed in staff meeting, because I've learned from experience that if you have three or four monkeys that look alike and talk to each other, they can be fed at staff meeting. Everybody is interested in those. But every now and then you will have a monkey that doesn't look like any other monkey, has nothing in common with the others, and it would be a waste of valuable time to feed it in a staff meeting. So two of the monkeys are being fed privately, and it says on my calendar: feed Keith's monkey No. 2 at 3:00, and feed Sam's monkey No. 7 at 3:30.

With my schedule in my head, I tackle all the things in my in-basket, and by 10 a.m., when I've taken care of all of those, I walk down the hallway. But being a pro, my purpose is now quite different. I'm not going through the office to feed monkeys. All my monkeys are on feeding schedules. I know they're going to be fed, so my mind is free to do what only I can do.

As before, I run into Ed, our manager of Shipping and Receiving. I am his boss, three levels removed. I look past him and, as before, I see that crate there. Of course I'm mad about it, but I don't tell Ed that. I bid Ed a good morning, and I reach inside my coat pocket and pull out my monkey-feeding schedule. I see that I have a time scheduled to review Shipping and Receiving procedures.

This gorilla is on the back of the superintendent who has responsibility for Shipping and Receiving (among other things), and who reports to me. I put the gorilla on his back. I have five superintendents reporting to me, and their backs are repositories where I place monkeys and gorillas. I have no business putting monkeys or gorillas on the backs of people at Ed's level.

(**NOTE:** It is a basic principle of organizational reality that senior managers are not supposed to make end runs around subordinate managers to give directives to the latter's subordinates without first informing those subordinate managers (the obvious exception being life-and-death emergencies). When this principle is violated, resulting in what is often called "skip-level supervision," it can cause confusion as to priorities, to say nothing of overworking the affected subordinates.)

Without saying another word to Ed, I call the appropriate superintendent, Roger. As the phone rings, Roger is sitting in his office, minding his own business. I say, "Good morning, Roger. With regard to your gorilla No. 9, entitled 'Shipping Room Procedures,' when was our next feeding time for that gorilla?" I know, of course, but I'm just testing him.

So he looks it up in his little black book and says, "Well, Bill, according to my schedule, we're feeding that one two weeks from now."

"Roger, I have news for you. We're feeding that gorilla tomorrow morning at 8:30 instead."

"Where are you calling from, boss?"

Faster than a Speeding Bullet

Within seconds, miraculously, Roger shows up in the Shipping Room. All the while, I'm serenely walking away from the Shipping Room back toward my office, perfectly happy to let human nature take its course. I know what's going to happen now. Roger hits the Shipping Room and says to Ed, "Was Oncken here?"

"Yes, he was here."

"Ah. What did he see?"

"I'm not really sure."

"Hmmm," said Roger, "that considerably enlarges the scope of the problem."

Roger gets hold of Ed's boss, who's the foreman, and the three of them huddle. And Roger says, "I've got a problem. Tomorrow morning at 8:30 I have to answer Oncken's question, 'How's it coming?' For monkeys I get five minutes, but for gorillas, I get a half hour; and Oncken will not be interested in how things are coming today, because by tomorrow that will be history, and Oncken is not an historian. He will want to know how it's coming tomorrow morning at 8:30. Therefore, we're going to have to get this place in the kind of shape that—when he asks me, 'How's it coming?'—I can tell him how's it coming as of right then. What did he see?"

What Was Impossible Before Is Easier Now

They looked around, and the first thing they saw was that crate. By some miracle, that crate was on a truck and out the gate within three minutes. Monday they couldn't ship it because the truck was up on jacks having the transmission fixed; Tuesday they couldn't do it because the truck was smashed and in the body shop; Wednesday they couldn't do it because they had some other rush orders and couldn't get a truck. People who work where the action is have an amazing ability to do the impossible once they make up their minds they want to do it. No one will ever know how it happens; that's their secret.

Then they went through the rest of the shipping room and turned the place upside down because they didn't know what else I might have seen, and they wanted the shipping room in proper shape to give me an acceptable, up-to-date report tomorrow morning at 8:30. They worked all night to bridge the gulf between how it is and how they want it to be when they report to me, and all of this activity was triggered by my routine visit.

At exactly 8:30 the next day, Roger walked into my office bleary-eyed. Me, I was rested; I had nine hours of sleep because I knew exactly what was happening. "How's it coming?" I asked. As he answered, I took a pad of paper and started writing down what he told me. Because I don't write fast, I told him to slow down and repeat some things. He knew why I was writing all of this down; when we were through, I was going down into the Shipping and Receiving Room, taking what he had told me as a checklist, to see for myself.

Let's Go See

When he had finished his briefing, I said to him, "Fine. Now let's go down and have a look at it." When we arrived on the scene at the Shipping Room, I was astounded. The whole appearance of the place had changed. The floors were swept, the crate was shipped, pallets were stacked in neat piles, and so it was throughout the entire place!

Do you see the difference between the results I got as an amateur and the results I have now? As an amateur, when I told Ed, "Get the crate shipped," what would have happened? The crate would have been shipped. But instead, as a pro, what did I do? I talked to my superintendent, right? What happened? The shipment of the crate was a trivial thing compared to everything else that happened. Since they didn't know what I saw, they took care of everything that three pairs of eyes could see, working all night long. So many self-assignments were created and executed I don't think I could ever calculate the leverage I had acquired by this; moreover, they learned a few things along the way about self-reliance and punctuality in carrying out their own responsibilities (in addition to what they learned about managerial follow-up by observing my personal example).

What About a No-Show?

As you recall, Rule 3 says, "Monkeys shall be fed on the responsibility of the subordinate, at the time and place specified in the feeding schedule; bosses shall not be chasing down starving monkeys and feeding them on the fly, catch-as-catch-can!" This sounds quite simple, but what if you get stood up at monkey feeding time? Your subordinate, Keith, is due in your office at 2 p.m. for monkey feeding, but he is a no-show. What then? Well, I'll play the role of the boss in this situation, and we will see what happens.

Keith is due in my office at 2:00. The appointed hour arrives, but no Keith. He just plain forgot the appointment. That can happen to anybody. However, technically, what do we call it since Keith is not here? Insubordination. Only he doesn't know this yet because he just forgot.

It is now 2:15. Keith still isn't here, and I am steamed! The next move was his—show up in my office for monkey feeding. He forgot the appointment and thus forced me into making the next move. No matter what happens, I now have the next move: ignore the problem, forget it, wait for him to remember, call him on the telephone, ask Sue (my secretary) to call him. What am I going to do?

If I were an amateur, I would remind Keith about the appointment, or I would have Sue remind him. But it was his responsibility to remember to be here, and if I remind him, I will have assumed his responsibility. You don't teach people to assume responsibility by taking responsibility away from them. Somehow, I must encourage his assuming responsibility while at the same time making the next move that he forced me to make.

So I ask Sue to call each of my managers to my office. They gather around the conference table, breathlessly waiting to find out what the crisis is so they can engage in self-sacrifice above and beyond the call of duty.

When everything is quiet, I say, "I've gathered you here together because we are faced with a crisis. Fifteen minutes ago I was stood up at monkey feeding time. Now, I tolerate human failing, first in myself and then in others; and that is why I will not name names, nor will I point fingers. But the crisis is so severe that I'm calling all of you together, even though only one person infracted. I am doing this in order to make sure that none of you will ever again do this thing. That's how important this is.

"I want to explain to you a condition of your employment. I thought I'd explained it before, but I want to repeat it. It is a condition of your employment that you show up at monkey feeding time. Have I made myself plain?" They allow what I have, so I say, "Meeting is dismissed."

They go out. As the others start interrogating each other to find out who did it, Keith—the culprit—is hanging back because he doesn't want it revealed that he was the one. Realizing he has a bit of unfinished business with me, he is busy looking for an opportunity to disengage himself from the group. He rushes down the hall, walks into my office, apologetic, and says, "Bill, I'm the one that did it to you; I'm awfully sorry, and I promise you I will never do it again."

"Keith," I reply, "Keith, buck up, old boy. All is not lost. After all, this could happen to anybody . . . once!"

It Is a Matter of Life and Death

Why am I so adamant? Because we are dealing in matters of life and death, the life and death of monkeys and gorillas. There's only one program that should come ahead of this in your company, and that is your safety program, where the life and death of human beings is at stake. But right after that comes the care and feeding of monkeys. We've got to discipline ourselves in this regard.

Why? Because at the end of the year when the people in the Accounting Department total up the annual results, draw that bottom line, and write the final figure under that bottom line, that figure is the vector sum of the activities of myriads of monkeys and gorillas.

If, during the year, a monkey or a gorilla occasionally starves to death now and then for lack of feeding, the accountants might never find it. On the other hand, if it is habitual practice to allow valuable monkeys and gorillas to starve to death for lack of feeding (this is called procrastination), then that bottom line figure will not be what it should be. Wish that condition on your competitors, but don't tolerate it in your own company!

The Fourth Rule

Monkey-feeding appointments may, in the case of conflict, be rescheduled at the suggestion of either party, but may never be indefinitely postponed; failure to make progress shall not be accepted as a reason for rescheduling feeding appointments.

There are times, of course, when monkey feeding has to be rescheduled, times when feeding the monkey might cost the company more than it could contribute.

Suppose, for example, that I am to feed Keith's monkey at 2 p.m. this afternoon, but at 9 a.m. Keith calls me and says, "Bill, I know that I am scheduled to be in your office at 2:00 to feed the

Rule 4

Make sure progress is made on the vital monkeys and gorillas.

monkey. However, I just got a call from one of our customers who claims that the parts we made for them do not fit the intended product. I would like to take some engineers and some of our sales-people down there to see if we can't resolve this problem. This will take all day, and since I cannot be in two places at once, I suggest that we re-schedule the feeding time of this monkey."

Should I accede? Well, of course! There is no way I am going to insist on meeting our original monkey-feeding schedule. If the feeding schedule is standing in the way of a contribution to corpo-rate goals and objectives, or if Keith encounters hail, sleet, high water, and other acts of God, re-schedule the feeding. But never reschedule appointments unilaterally (that would be bad manners as well as poor communications); re-schedule them bilaterally.

Lack of Progress Is No Excuse

Re-scheduling appointments for good rea-sons is one thing, but suppose Keith calls me at 9 a.m. regarding the scheduled 2 p.m. monkey feeding, saying, "Bill, I could be there at two; I've got nothing else scheduled. However, I've been terribly busy. I have been unable to do anything about this monkey. Therefore, at two I will have nothing to report. I would hate to waste even five minutes of your valuable time, Oncken, with nothing to report. Therefore, out of consideration for you, I suggest that we re-schedule the monkey feeding time to another day when I have made sufficient progress to make the meeting worthwhile."

How would you react to this request? I would say to him, "Of course I know that you're short-handed and overworked, and I can understand your not having made any progress. For the fact that you have made no progress, you are generously forgiven in advance. I practice the Biblical Golden Rule, but that is beside the point. For the monkey to survive, it must be fed, so be here at 2:00!"

Keith is astonished. He says, "Wait a minute, Oncken, what would I talk about if I've made no progress? How can I talk about nothing?"

"Easy. It's done in three parts. First, you explain exactly what the state of affairs would have been if you had made progress. Secondly, you explain what the state of affairs is right now, being as how you haven't made any progress. You subtract the second one from the first and talk about the difference. Right? That's the no-progress report, and I am insisting on it because lack of progress is just as significant to this company as progress!"

Do Something, Or....

Keith is dazed. He does not know what hit him. Never before has he made a no-progress report, and as the morning wears on, the prospect of making this one nauseates him. He is now faced with two unpleasant courses of action: make no progress or do something. Which of the two will he regard as being least unpleasant? Doing something. Certainly it will be unpleasant to do something, but that will be less unpleasant than doing nothing and making a lack-of-progress report.

At 2 p.m. he shows up in my office, grinning from ear to ear with deep self-satisfaction. He says, "Hi, Oncken. Surprise! I've done something."

This is called the motivation of people.

The President's Gorilla

Notice that the president of your company has surrendered his right to re-schedule feeding times. Every year, your president leads the master gorilla of them all by a golden chain out onto a stage; it is called the annual shareholders' meeting. All day long at this meeting, the shareholders ask your president, "How's it coming?" in many different ways, and the president explains the progress of the past year.

Can you imagine what would happen if, one month before the meeting, the president realized that the company had made no progress and sent a letter to all the shareholders explaining that since no progress had been made, he was postponing the meeting until six months later? There would be a flood of telephone calls, letters, and telegrams saying, "Ready or not, Mr. President, we're coming. We're going to feed the gorilla!"

If your president has surrendered his right to reschedule feeding appointments, then who are you to be any different? Anyone in the company who aspires to be president should now get accustomed to the requirements of the presidency so that the shock will not be so great when the time comes. The best time to start developing people into presidents is the day they walk in the door.

This all goes back to a basic leadership principle which states that accountability shall always be rendered by date, and never by readiness. This is essential to the concept of stewardship. It is one thing to be late on the completion date of a project, but it is quite another to skip accountability for the process itself.

We all miss a completion date every now and then; so, the date will have to be re-scheduled. But feeding dates are not re-scheduled simply for lack of progress. I will rate my people as much on what I hear during the feeding sessions as on whether or not they made a completion date that was established 12 months ago without the benefit of clairvoyance.

After all, if they are two months late in completing the project, but what I learned in feeding sessions told me that the situation would have been worse if they hadn't performed heroic feats given the unforeseen obstacles thrown in their path, they deserve some consideration for that!

The Fifth Rule

Monkeys shall be fed face to face whenever possible; otherwise by telephone, but never by mail. Memoranda, email, faxes, and reports must be used at times in the feeding process, but cannot substitute for face-to-face dialogue.

Suppose that the day you get back to work after having learned the first four **Rules for the Care and Feeding of Monkeys and Gorillas,** you walk down the hallway and spot one of your subordinates, Sam, advancing toward you. As he approaches, you know what his opener will be. And you can't wait to see the shock on his face when he hears your response.

Sure enough, he says to you, "Hi boss, we've got a problem." You then respond, "Sam, 'we' have never had a problem, and if I have anything to say about it, 'we' will never again have a problem; it is either yours or mine, but it is not ours. So the first thing we need to do is neaten up the pronouns a bit and find out whose problem it is. If it turns out to be yours, I'll be glad to help you with it. And if the problem turns out to be mine, I hope you will help me. But it is not our problem. Now, what's the problem?"

He now realizes that the problem is his, at least for the time being, but he is an experienced manager who doesn't give up the fight easily. He will use every wile at his disposal to make sure you wind up with the next move. So for half an hour, he explains the problem to you in obfuscating, ambiguous terms, until finally you know less about the problem than you did before he opened his mouth.

You don't know whose problem it is, yours or his; you don't even know what the problem is; you don't even know what the next move is. Half an hour has gone by, and you can't spend any more time there, so you say to him, "Bob, awfully glad

Rule 5

Avoid being misunderstood.

you raised that point. We've been here half an hour and barely scratched the surface on it. We need a decision on this."

Bob is strongly in agreement. "Do we ever," he says.

"Tell you what," you reply, "would you please reduce to writing all that you said here and include anything else you think relevant? Please lay it all out there in not more than one page and send it to me."

"Okay," Bob says, a little surprised because you have never done this to him before.

The two of you walk away, and you are grinning from ear to ear, congratulating yourself. "Bob has the next move—to write a memo."

And then that afternoon you walk by Bob's office, and you stick your head in and say, "Hi, Bob, how's it coming?" And I'll tell you, years are coming off your life.

Bob Has the Next Move (So You Think)

The next morning, you show up at your office. At 8:45 the inter-office mail brings you Bob's memo. You read it, and by the time you get down to his signature, whose next move is it? Yours! No question about it. Even if the next move is to think about it, file it, ignore it, or tear it up and throw it away, you've got it! This means, of course, that any memo you get from your subordinates automatically puts you in what role with regard to the memo—the worker role or supervisory role? Worker! Bob is now in the supervisory role.

Ten minutes after you finish reading the memo, Bob walks by your office, sticks his head in the door and says, "Hi, boss. Did you get my memo?" You see. He is exercising his supervisory role.

"Yes, I got it," you answer, thankful you can give a good report to your supervisor.

"Did you read it?"

"Yes, I read it."

"What are you doing about it?" he demands to know, and with that you are right back in the same shape you were before.

Controlling Paper/Email Monkeys from Your Staff

What went wrong? Were you mistaken to ask him for a memo? Of course not. There are scores of perfectly good reasons why you ask for a memorandum. Documentation, future reference, refresh your memory, goodness only knows what. That part is all right, but what should you have said instead of "Send me a memo"? You should have said, "Bring it to me."

Let's play the whole scene that way and see what happens.

The next morning you come to work, and Bob walks in to bring you his memo. He turns around to walk out, and you say to him, "Hey, Bob, wait a minute. Come back here. Sit down. I will never again read a memo in isolation."

A memo is one-half dialogue; a monkey is whatever the next move is when dialogue between two people breaks off. When a person writes you a memo and signs his name, you've got the next move. That's how simple it is. Therefore, if he writes you a memo, sit him down and resume the dialogue, because as long as you have him talking, there's a fighting chance that the next move could be his.

Thus, you say to him, "Bob, is this your signature at the bottom of this memo?"

"Yes."

"That means you wrote this memo?"

"Yes."

"Good. Would you please read the memo to me?"

"Read it to you? I wrote it!"

"Which means you are the most qualified to read it. I want you to read it so that I will be freed up to interrupt you with Kipling's famous Six Servants: what, why, who, how, where, and when."

These six words are indispensable tools in the hands of any manager who must defend himself against being deceived by an honest man. I don't mean that Bob would really deceive me; he's not that kind of an individual. He is, however, a keen student of history, and a prudent man as well. He knows that when you write a memo to anybody else in the company, the minute said memo goes through a printer or is sent by email, it suddenly becomes quotable. It becomes official. And he's had many regrettable experiences in the past when he's written an innocent memo to his boss or to somebody else, and four weeks later that memo got in the hands of the most unlikely individual who misunderstood it, misquoted it, and started administrative brush fires. So, whenever he writes a memo to anybody now, Bob writes it in such a way that he will never be misunderstood, never be misquoted.

How do you write an inter-office memo in such a way it will never be misunderstood? You use the technique that lawyers for centuries have perfected. You write something nobody can understand; then nobody can misunderstand it. That is, you can't misunderstand anything if you don't understand it in the first place. So he uses the technique of double-talk. What he really wants to say is not in that memo at all. It's between the lines.

Therefore, don't waste your time reading his memo. Have him read it to you. That way you find out what's between the lines—and that's what you really want to know. As you talk, he's perfectly willing to tell you what he means because the walls don't have ears, the place isn't bugged; this is eyeball-to-eyeball dialogue. Get this thing out in the open. The memo just provides guidelines as to what you are talking about.

More real communicating and understanding will occur in 15 minutes of dialogue with Bob than will ever occur if you try to save time and spend five minutes reading the memo.

The only time I feel anything should be put down on paper is when documentation is an important consideration; but don't use paper or email either to transmit or create understanding.

Dialogue is the only thing that can do it. If, after reaching an understanding, you want to document it, then you can dictate a memo for the file, and the memo will contain documentation of understandings already reached through dialogue.

While Bob is sitting in your office in dialogue with you, you get a good feel for the essence of his message. Finally, you both realize that the dialogue has passed the point of diminishing returns, so Bob says, "I've got to get back to work."

"No," you say, "the next item on the agenda is for you and me to figure out how the next move might be yours."

"Well, I'm bushed, boss. So we need to figure out the next move in 30 minutes."

"That does give you a problem, but one I will gladly help you with."

Because Bob wants to be out of your office in the next 30 minutes, he will display great creativity, imagination, drive, and enthusiasm trying to find some meaningful next move that you will allow him to make. Necessity is still the mother of creativity and invention.

This brings us, then, to a restatement of our fifth rule:

Rule 5: *Monkeys shall be fed face to face whenever possible; otherwise by telephone, but never by mail. Memoranda, email, faxes, and reports must be used at times in the feeding process, but cannot substitute for face-to-face dialogue.*

If the Next Move Is Yours?

One question that arises from the practice of face-to-face dialogue is this: What course do you follow if the dialogue ends and it is clear that the next substantive move belongs to you? For example, during a dialogue with one of your subordinates, suppose the two of you identify the next move as "touch base with the financial vice president." The question then becomes, Who should make the next move—you or your subordinate?

You know Bob wants you to touch base with the financial vice president, and the excuse Bob uses is that the financial vice president jealously guards what he—the VP—perceives to be the protocols and status differentials that go with his senior position, and these don't permit Bob to directly interface with him. Bob explains all of that to you.

He's probably right in his perception of the situation, but Bob is setting you up. You are supposed to go in and talk to the financial vice president. And when you leave the financial vice president's office, who will be waiting for you outside with the question, "How's it coming?" Bob will, of course, and that means that—once again—he will have the supervisory role, and you will have the worker role!

So you say to him, "Bob, I'm well aware of our corporate customs and the status sensibilities of vice president. And I know it would make our vice president nervous and insult his ego if you went in there alone, but that does not get you off the hook. You will go in to see him anyway, but I will come along with you. However, we are going to pull the thing off in such a way that the vice president will think you are coming along with me, but you and I will not be mixed up on that point, will we?"

"No, sir!" says Bob.

You and Bob go together to see the vice president, but where is the monkey? On Bob's back! You walk in the vice president's office with the monkey on Bob's back, and you leave with the monkey on Bob's back.

It is unconscionable how many higher-level management people are running errands for lower-level people just because of status differentials, and then the lower level people are saying, "How's it coming?" "Got to get off the pot." "Fish or cut bait." Take your subordinate with you. It is often regarded as very good management development practice, and that way, the monkey will never leap.

Every Monkey Has a Home Room

Every monkey has a home room, and that is why they don't all wind up at the bottom of the organization. Some belong to you, others to your boss, others to your subordinates. But when monkeys get lost, they have no instincts for returning to home rooms. When a monkey is lost, it impulsively wants to climb. It just wants to go up, not go home. So monkeys are constantly climbing, and because of the vertical pyramidal nature of most organizations, you've got hundreds of monkeys heading for a very small space called corporate headquarters. That is why most people regard corporate headquarters as the single biggest bottleneck of the entire organization. Why? Because of all the monkeys climbing in there. The people in the field will tell you, "Don't send anything to headquarters unless you want to just kiss it goodbye. You'll never hear from it again." And I say to people in the field, "Don't send anything into headquarters which would hurt you at all if nothing ever happened."

The fact that a monkey belongs in your home room does not preclude your subordinates' babysitting the monkey, filing the monkey in their files, or giving you ideas on how to handle the monkey.

The Sixth Rule

Memos, email, or reports running to several pages or more shall be covered by a synopsis of one page or less to facilitate instant dialogue.

The fifth rule suggested that you engage your subordinates in dialogue over their reports, emails, and memos.

But suppose that tomorrow, when you arrive at your office, you find large, 35-page report that Bob, one of your subordinates, spent three months working on. This report comes complete with enclosures and attachments containing bar graphs, pie charts, extrapolated exponential curves, and tables of correlation—a veritable master's thesis. Are you going to dialogue that thing away? Impossible! What, therefore, do you do?

147

My suggestion is to call the person up, hand him back the report, and ask him, "When will you be back with a one-page summary of this?" That will blow his mind!

When he comes back, he's got that one-page summary clipped on top of his 35-page report. He doesn't want you to forget that report; he sweated blood over that thing. He hands them both to you. You keep the one-page summary and toss the report back in his lap. You read the first sentence on the one-page summary, and, finding it utterly incomprehensible, you say, "Bob, I don't understand that first sentence."

"Boss," says he, "this 35-page report cannot be summarized in one page. That first sentence summarizes the first 19 pages in that report, and you can never understand that first sentence unless you read the first 19 pages."

"Well, Bob, you've got the report. Read me the first 19 pages."

"Don't be silly, boss. I don't have to read you those pages. I can tell you about them in a fraction of the time it would take me to read them to you."

And so he tells you about it, and by interrogating him with who, how, why, what, where, and when, you get the central thrust of what this is all about.

Bob pulls his chair up alongside you, shows you the graphs and the charts, and uses his finger to point out various things. After 30 minutes, you have a more thorough understanding of what that report is about than you ever would if you

Rule 6

*Facilitate
instant dialogue.*

had sat in the solitude of your den and struggled through unfamiliar material by yourself.

When you're through with all of it, you say to him, "Bob, this time was very profitable."

As Bob gets up as if to leave, you say, "Wait a minute, Bob. Aren't you forgetting something?"

"No. I don't think so. What is it?"

"Your 35-page report."

"But that is yours, boss. It has your name on it. It's addressed to you."

"That may be true, but that's no reason for me to keep it. Would you please take it with you, and on your way out, tell Sue, my assistant, that you have it. She will then make a note for her computer files which tells her everything that belongs to me that is filed elsewhere."

The report will be filed in his files. If it were in my file, chances are I would forget where it is. But now that Bob has it, I always know where it is. If the report is in my cabinet and I can't find it, that is called procrastination. But if it's in his cabinet and he can't find it when I need it, that is insubordination. And finally, as long as the report is in his cabinet, it is just conceivable that he might do something with it!

So, lengthy reports should always be accompanied by a short summary of what is in the report. The short summary facilitates dialogue, enabling you to quickly get a feel for what the report is about. Longer reports without the short summary have to be read and digested before the dialogue is meaningful. The primary purpose of the dialogue is to identify substantive **next moves** that should be made while you are reading the report, thus eliminating a bottleneck while you read this report.

Business must be activity oriented. Without cause, there is no effect. Without activity, there will be no results. A mere commitment to results will accomplish no more than New Year's resolutions, and they have a lousy track record.

And yet, some people have a mystical belief that if they are deeply committed to something, their commitment alone will make it happen. People who emphasize objectives but ignore activities lose sight of the scientific principle of cause and effect. They regard objectives as causes and results as effects.

It's one thing to be committed to a result nine months from now; it's another to be committed to taking specific next moves today or tomorrow that improve the odds of attaining those results. A commitment to an objective can't be an effective cause of a result. Only those activities that are directed toward the attainment of the objective can be effective.

Managers correctly commit themselves to objectives and goals whose target dates lie in the future. But if they leave unstated what the specific next moves are—the specific current actions designed to contribute to any desired end—they court failure. When they state these next moves, and when

these actions are expressed in quantitative terms,
ambiguity in performance requirements is virtually eliminated. And performance improves.

Epilogue

You've seen the many different ways you can pick up monkeys. How easy it is to get them. You can accumulate monkeys by the dozens without realizing it, so that by the end of the day, you've got a desk top crawling with monkeys you've received from your subordinates. But at this point you might be saying to yourself, "What other choice do I have? I manage things. I supervise people. Collecting monkeys is my job." Well, sometimes that's true, but not always.

You've seen monkey mismanagement, as practiced by amateur managers, and exactly how professionals manage their monkey populations.

Remember, a monkey is whatever the next move is when dialogue between two parties breaks off. It is not a problem. A monkey is not a project. A monkey is not a program. It is a next move within a project, a program, or a problem. That's all a monkey is. And for every monkey there are two parties involved, namely one to work it and one to supervise it.

Monkey mismanagement begins whenever you say to an individual working for you, "Let me think it over, and I'll let you know." What you have just done is accepted responsibility from that individual and promised him or her a progress report.

You accept responsibility from your boss, and you promise your boss a progress report. If you do that with a subordinate, you have, in effect, made your subordinate the boss on that issue. You've made yourself that person's subordinate. If you accept responsibility from someone and promise that person a progress report, that gives him or her the right to check up. And checking up is a management—not a "worker"—responsibility.

So when you accept monkeys from your people, two things happen. One, you allow your people to supervise you. And two, you prevent them from getting on with their jobs. Think about that second point for a minute. How do you feel when you can't make any progress because you're waiting for someone else to make a decision, to get back to you, to give you the information you need? Frustrated, right? Well, so do your people.

And frustrated, angry people don't make the most productive, quality-minded workers. So you should be concerned about their frustration. You should also be concerned about what's happening to you. You're becoming "one big bottleneck." If you promise enough things to enough people and don't keep any of them, you're going to feel guilty.

And that's just the beginning of a vicious cycle. You feel guilty, so you take on more monkeys; your people get more frustrated, and you feel even guiltier. How do you break the cycle? By remembering that doing your staff's work for them isn't your job. The real purpose of your job is to provide the fuel to enable others to perform at their best. This is what we refer to as **The Care and Feeding of Monkeys**.

It's a system to help empower your people and successfully manage your monkey population.

Let's quickly summarize some of the key points.

You have seen that, while you can decide to let any particular monkey live, you must guard against allowing too many monkeys to survive.

If your monkey population becomes too big, some of them are likely to end up on your back. Not all monkeys need to survive. Some can—and should—be shot or allowed to die a natural death.

So your first step is to decide if a monkey is worth anyone's time. Is a project or proposal feasible? Is it something that has to be done? Should you do it yourself? Should one of your people do it? Or should it be done by someone else in the company? These are the questions you have to ask yourself every time you encounter a monkey.

And once you make the decision to feed a monkey, you must continue asking questions. Is this monkey still worth feeding or should it be shot? Keep in mind that those monkeys you choose to feed have a way of multiplying.

So don't take on more monkeys than you can handle. If you take on too many monkeys, you won't be able to feed them all. The negative impact for you is that you'll have a lot of hungry and neglected monkeys hanging around. Instead of having a number of successes, you face the possibility of a lot of failures. Why? Because you simply won't have enough time or energy to get any of your projects done well. For the organization, the negative impact is gridlock.

Instead of trying to do it all yourself, instead of having a pack of screaming, hungry monkeys running around wild, you must delegate safely to your people, using **Oncken's Monkey Management System**. We have a method to get you into that position. It's the monkey management system. Before you can delegate, you must understand the twin arts of coaching and assigning. When you learn to delegate, you are able to control monkeys and keep them all healthy.

But some managers are uncomfortable about giving managees too much responsibility for monkeys. In fact, the greatest obstacle to building self-reliance in your people may be your fear of what they might do when "carrying the ball." That's why, for every monkey that leaves your presence, you assign a level of freedom. The **Oncken Freedom Scale** now becomes a risk management tool. While ensuring that the monkey stays on the subordinate's back by outlawing the use of Freedom Levels 1 and 2, you give no more freedom of action than the your anxieties will permit—and that will vary with the issues and circumstances. Depending on the subordinate and the issue, you could maintain a very short leash indeed (Freedom Level 3).

The message here is to coach effectively, because coaching is the development of people. You can't just dump monkeys. You must first make sure your staff members can handle them. That's the secret of **Oncken's Freedom Scale**—

giving people only as much responsibility and freedom of action as they can handle. Let them do the work. But be around when they need you to help with the feedings.

Some managees will be more capable of caring for monkeys than others at first. But as you work with your people, you'll help all of them develop the ability to recognize a problem or opportunity, recommend a solution, and follow through with specific next moves.

Using the **Oncken Monkey Management System**, you offer people the opportunity for growth and increased responsibility—and you pave the way to safe and effective delegation. You also provide yourself with the time you need to do what you're supposed to be doing.

So, keep the monkeys with your staff, and don't inadvertently accept a monkey without realizing it. Monkeys can be sneaky. They can find ways to bounce back at you when you least expect it.

Always schedule a follow-up appointment whenever a monkey is given to someone. This allows you to minimize unforeseen interruptions and keep control of your daily schedule. It's a very useful way to manage monkeys and make sure they remain with their proper owner.

*   *   *

Everything in this book has been aimed at teaching you how to control the timing and content of what you do in your staff relationships. Now that you have learned how to take control of the monkey population by using Oncken's time management strategies, you're going to be able to recognize a monkey coming at you from a distance and—most important—keep it off your back if it doesn't belong there.

About the Author

William Oncken, III received his MBA from Southern Methodist University in 1976, followed by several years in the insurance and estate planning industry. Prior to SMU, he served in Vietnam and then graduated from Texas A&M University in 1971. Bill joined the William Oncken Corporation in 1978 as Manager of Product Development. In 1985 he was appointed President under William Oncken, Jr., chairman, CEO, and creator of the Oncken propriety training programs, including the famous *Managing Management Time*™ seminar with his legendary "monkey-on-the-back" analogy. This program, now in its 40th year, enjoys international success with all levels of management. Bill succeeded his father, the late William Oncken, Jr., in February 1988 as CEO of the corporation. The unique philosophy of Oncken's internationally known seminar,

Managing Management Time™, became—over the years—an integral part of the cultures of scores of organizations, including Intel, Hewlett-Packard, Florida Power & Light, IBM, Milliken, Invacare, Western Digital, the Chicago Tribune, and several U.S. government agencies.

A gifted writer and articulator of issues of general management concern, Bill is frequently a keynote speaker for conferences, and he conducts training programs for corporations. His articles have appeared in several professional publications, including *Executive Excellence* and *SUCCESS* magazines.

About The William Oncken Corporation

Headquartered in Mesquite, Texas, a suburb of Dallas, The William Oncken Corporation has been providing business education to industry and government since 1960.

Key program offerings include: *Managing Management Time™*, *Managing Managerial Initiative™*, and *Communications in Management*.

For 40 years its flagship two-day seminar, *Managing Management Time™*, has been teaching professionals how to transform themselves into effective leaders. Using the "molecule of management" to illustrate organizational relationships, this timeless philosophy demonstrates why and how leadership, teamwork, planning, responsibility, and accountability begin with each individual (each "YOU") in your organization.

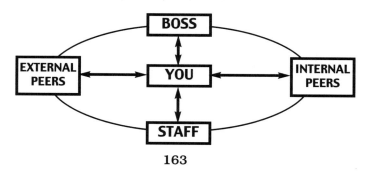

The classic 1974 *Harvard Business Review* article "Management Time: Who's Got the Monkey?"—excerpted from this seminar—deals with the responsibilities managers have in their relationship with their staff. *Monkey Business* is a more expansive treatment of that material, and is the first in a planned series of books that will deal with relationships inherent in organizational molecules.

The company's schedule of public seminar dates and locations is available on its Web site: www.oncken.com.

For details concerning an on-site presentation at your organization—be it a keynote speech, a one-on-one executive coaching session, or a customized seminar—contact the company directly.

The William Oncken Corporation
18601 LBJ FWY, Suite 520
Mesquite, Texas 75150

Phone: 972-613-2084
Fax: 972-613-3182
Email: Onckencorp@aol.com
Web site: www.oncken.com

DEVELOPMENT TOOLS FROM
EXECUTIVE EXCELLENCE PUBLISHING

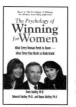

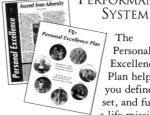